His Name

It is above all other names.
There is no name like His.

The names of God show us His nature.
We may wonder about who God is and no matter
what this world says, He is true to His names
found in scripture.

So many things happen in this life,
But He never changes.

He is the same yesterday, today, and tomorrow.

Search after Him, and find Him for He is there.

He loves you!

MY NAME

My name has the letters:
(Color the letters of your name.)

A B C D E F G H I J
K L M N O P Q R
S T U V W X Y Z

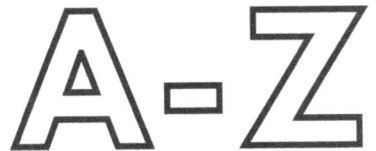

A-Z

LIST ALL THE NAMES OF GOD IN THE ABC'S YOU KNOW RIGHT NOW

a _____

b _____

c _____

d _____

e _____

f _____

g _____

h _____

i _____

j _____

k _____

l _____

m _____

n _____

o _____

p _____

q _____

r _____

s _____

t _____

u _____

v _____

w _____

x _____

y _____

z _____

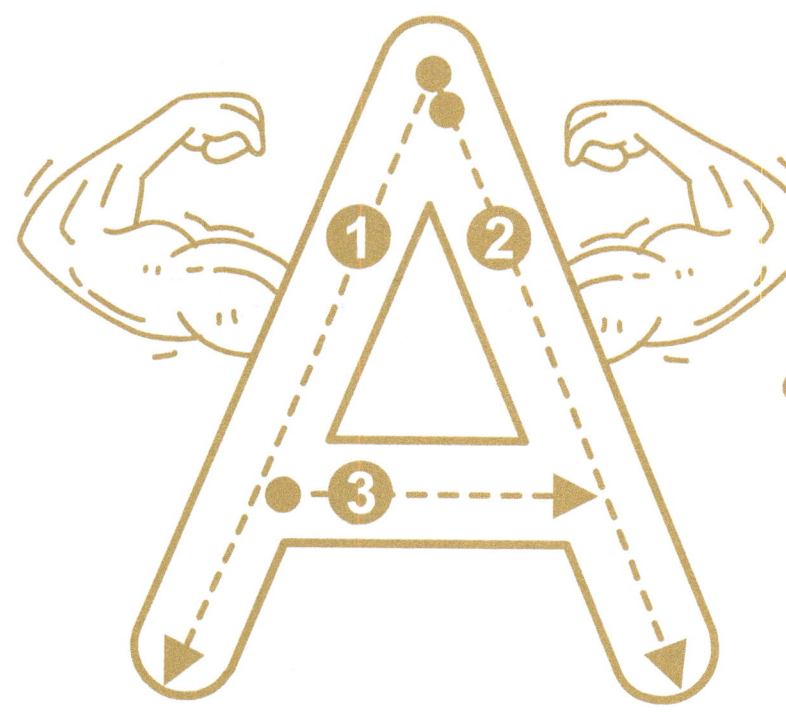

Revelation 1:8 (KJV)

8) I am Alpha and Omega, the beginning and the ending, saith the Lord, which is, and which was, and which is to come, the Almighty.

Almighty

Find all the letters A

A	B	C	A	D
A	F		A	D
A		A		A
H				A
V	A	S	A	D
A	A	V	S	A
A	F	M	D	A

Psalm 29:2 (KJV)
2) Give unto the Lord the glory due unto his name; worship the Lord in the beauty of holiness.

Adonai

(Lord, and signifying sovereignty)

Find all the letters a

a	b	c	a	d
a	f		d	a
a		**a**		a
h				a
v	a	s	a	d
a	a	v	s	a
a	f	m	d	a

John 6:35 (KJV)

35) And Jesus said unto them, I am the bread of life: he that cometh to me shall never hunger; and he that believeth on me shall never thirst.

Bread of Life

Find all the letters B

B	A	C	B	D
B	F		D	B
B		B		B
J				B
V	F	H	L	B
D	G	B	B	A
A	O	M	D	B

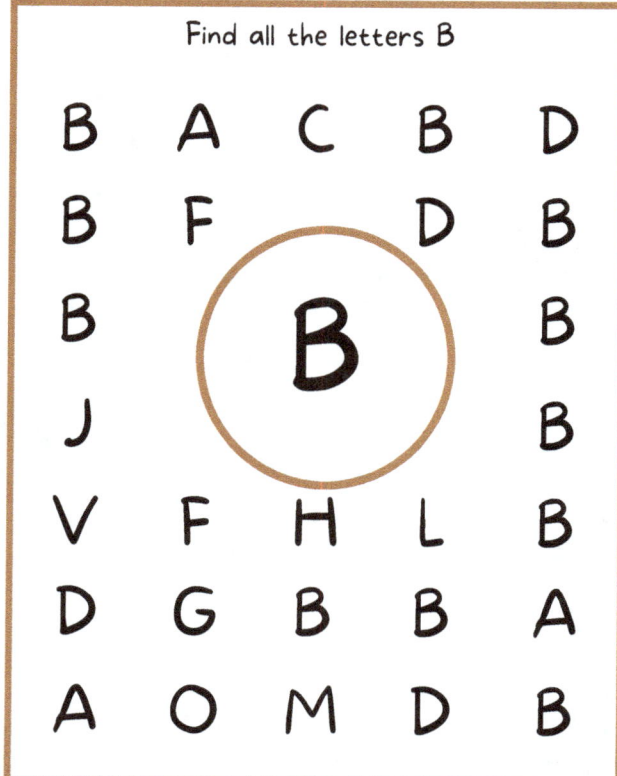

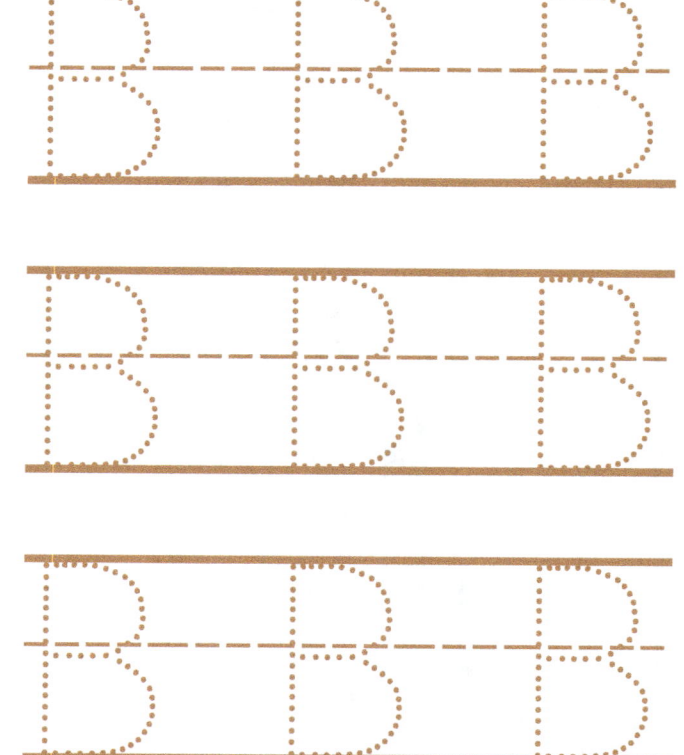

Revelation 22:13 (KJV)

13) I am Alpha and Omega, the beginning and the end, the first and the last.

FINISH

The Begining and the End

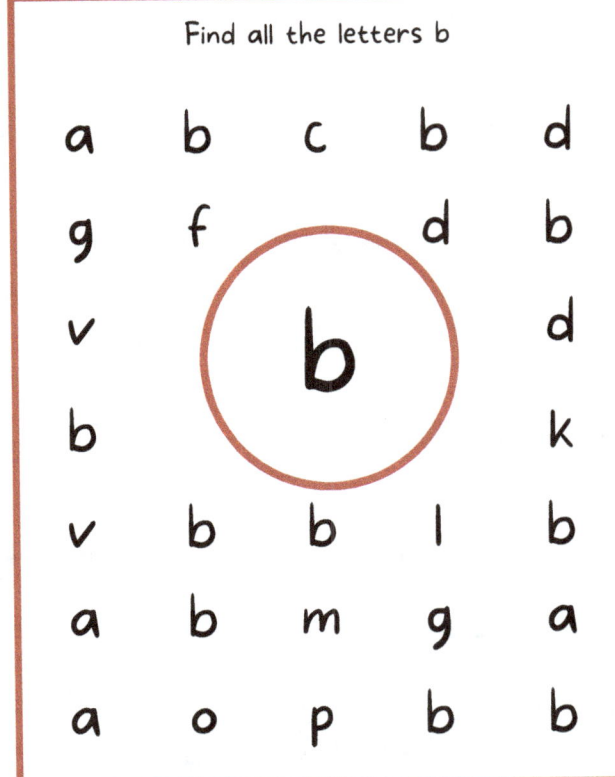

Find all the letters b

a	b	c	b	d
g	f		d	b
v		b		d
b				k
v	b	b	l	b
a	b	m	g	a
a	o	p	b	b

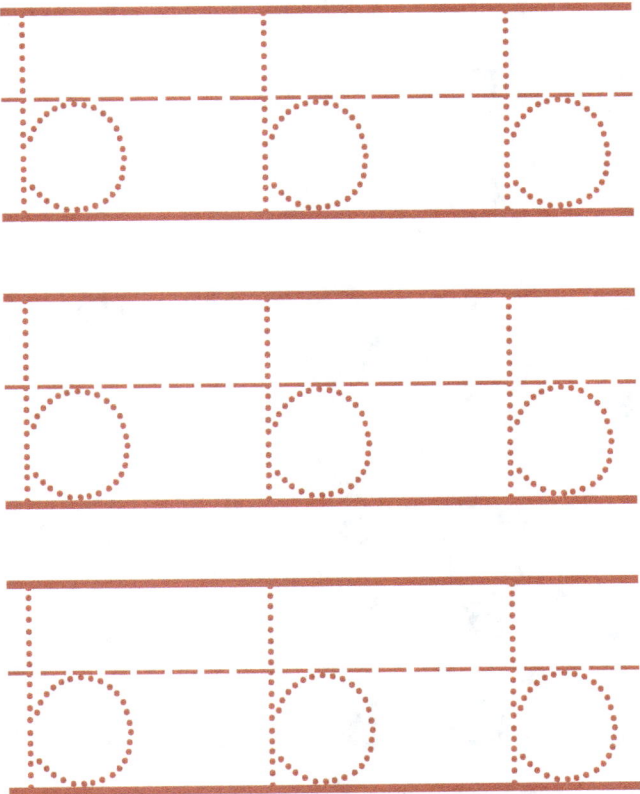

Cornerstone

1 Peter 2:7 (KJV)

7) Unto you therefore which believe he is precious: but unto them which be disobedient, the stone which the builders disallowed, the same is made the head of the corner.

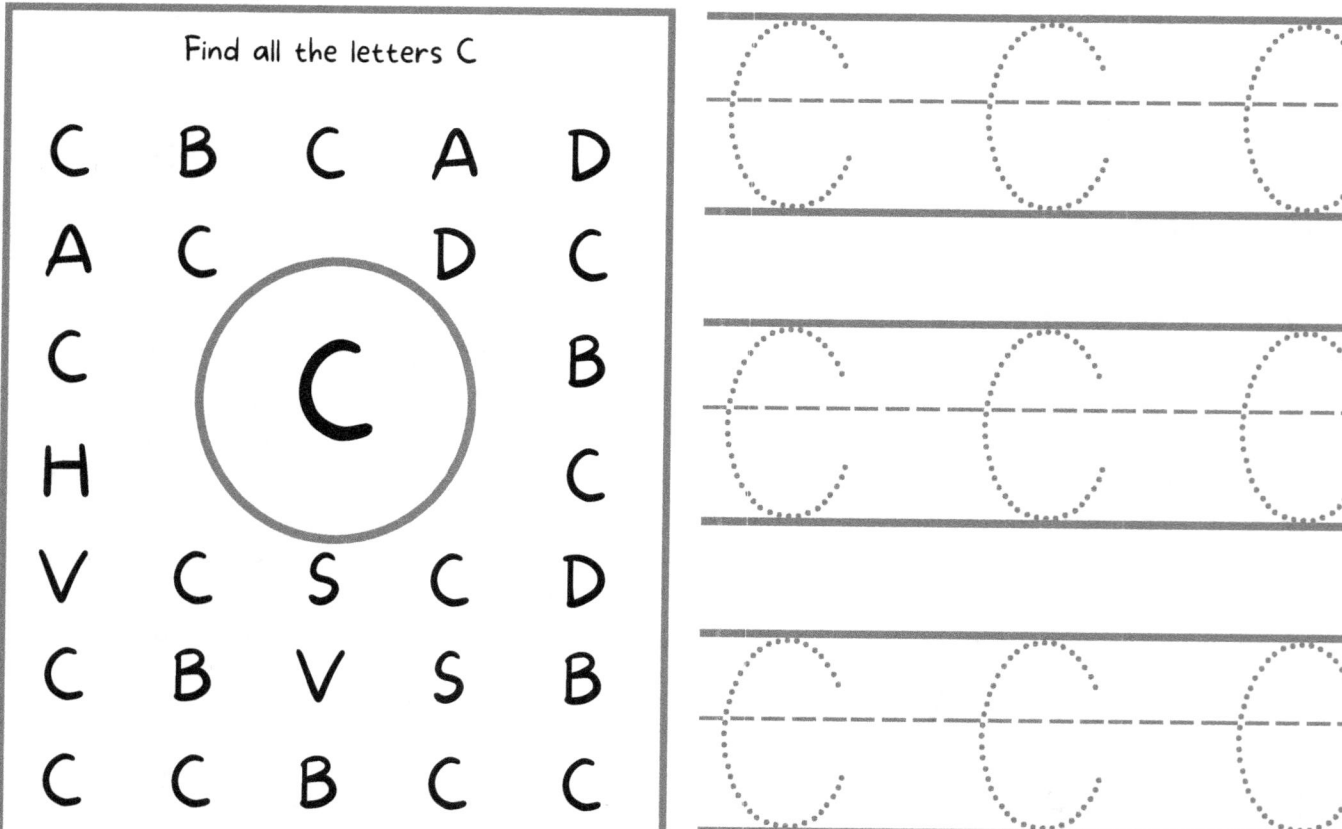

Find all the letters C

C	B	C	A	D
A	C		D	C
C		C		B
H				C
V	C	S	C	D
C	B	V	S	B
C	C	B	C	C

26) But the Comforter, which is the Holy Ghost, whom the Father will send in my name, he shall teach you all things, and bring all things to your remembrance, whatsoever I have said unto you. **John 14:26 (KJV)**

Comforter

Find all the letters c

c	b	c	e	f
c	c		z	n
c				m
j		C		c
p	y	c	c	s
o	c	l	c	v
k	g	b	d	c

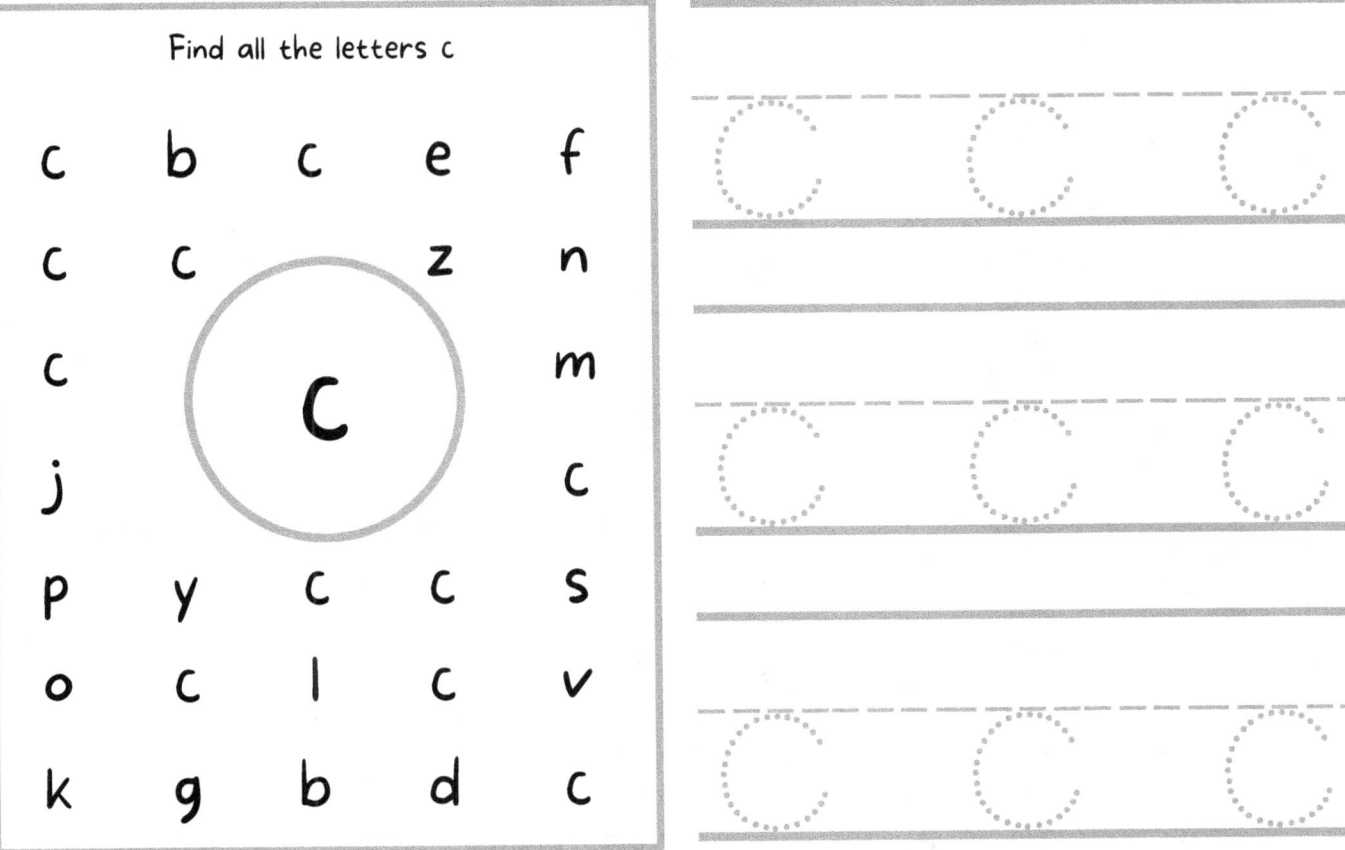

2) The Lord is my rock, and my fortress, and my deliverer; my God, my strength, in whom I will trust; my buckler, and the horn of my salvation, and my high tower.
Psalm 18:2 (KJV)

Deliverer

Find all the letters D

D	B	D	A	D
D	C		D	D
C		D		B
H				C
D	A	S	V	D
C	B	D	S	D
D	C	D	C	C

9) I am the door: by me if any man enter in, he shall be saved, and shall go in and out, and find pasture.
John 10:9 (KJV)

The Door

Find all the letters d

d	b	d	a	d
d	c		d	d
c		d		b
h				c
d	a	s	v	d
c	b	d	s	d
d	c	d	c	c

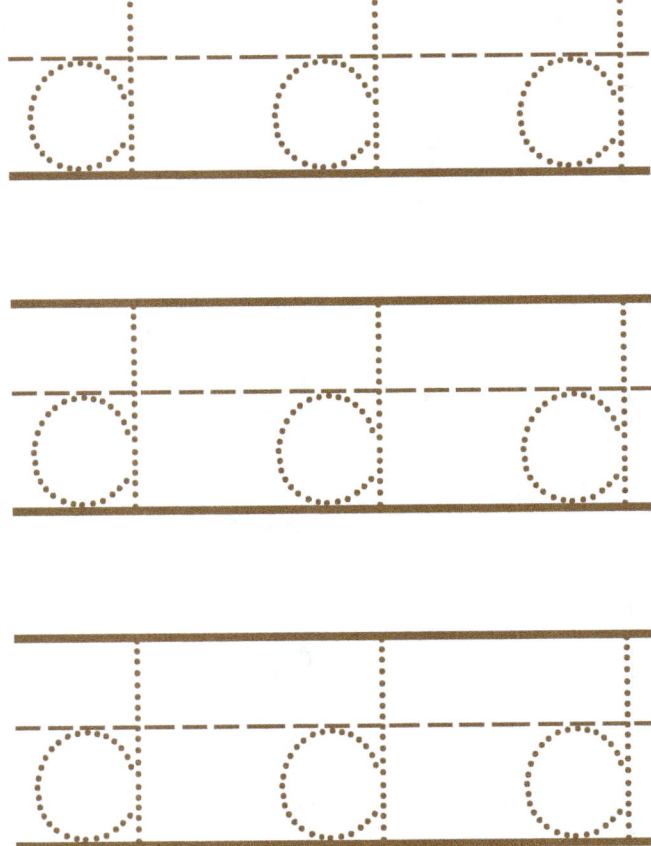

10) But the Lord is the true God, he is the living God, and an everlasting king: at his wrath the earth shall tremble, and the nations shall not be able to abide his indignation. **Jeremiah 10:10 (KJV)**

Everlasting King

Find all the letters E

E	B	D	E	D
D	C		D	D
E		E		B
H				E
E	A	S	E	D
C	B	D	S	E
E	C	E	E	C

3) And God Almighty bless thee, and make thee fruitful, and multiply thee, that thou mayest be a multitude of people; **Genesis 28:3 (KJV)**

El Shaddai
(God Almighty)

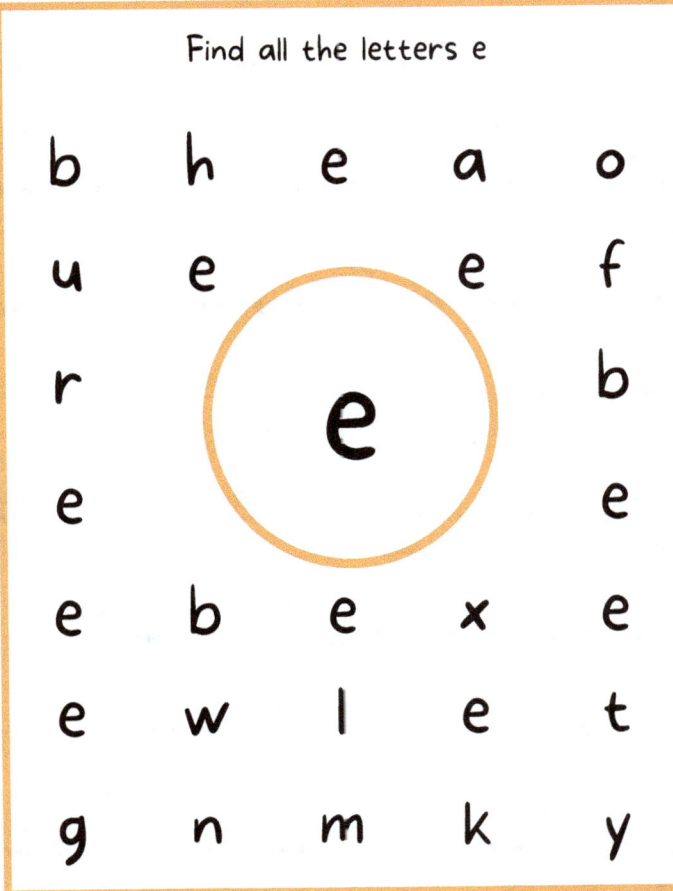

Find all the letters e

b	h	e	a	o
u	e			f
r		e		b
e				e
e	b	e	x	e
e	w	l	e	t
g	n	m	k	y

Ephesians 4:6 (KJV)

6) One God and Father of all, who is above all, and through all, and in you all.

God The Father

Find all the letters F

F	A	I	N	F
T	K	R		F
F		F		B
E				U
F	S	N	L	U
E	C	F	A	F
G	G	F	M	E	P

2) Looking unto Jesus the author and finisher of our faith; who for the joy that was set before him endured the cross, despising the shame, and is set down at the right hand of the throne of God. **Hebrews 12:2 (KJV)**

The Founder & Perfecter of our Faith

Find all the letters f

j	l	o	u	f
h	i		f	s
f		**f**		b
f				f
w	s	x	f	g
a	f	c	a	n
y	k	f	e	f

Gentle Whisper

12) ...And after the earthquake a fire; but the Lord was not in the fire: and after the fire a still small voice...
1 Kings 19:12 (KJV)

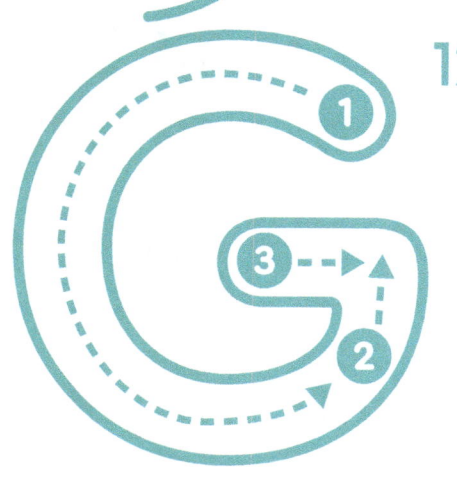

Find all the letters G

K	J	B	G	S
G	G			F	Q
L		**G**		B
U				B
X	M	N	D	F
A	F	G	G	G
W	L	G	E	N
				F

John 10:11 (KJV)

11) I am the good shepherd: the good shepherd giveth his life for the sheep.

Good Shepherd

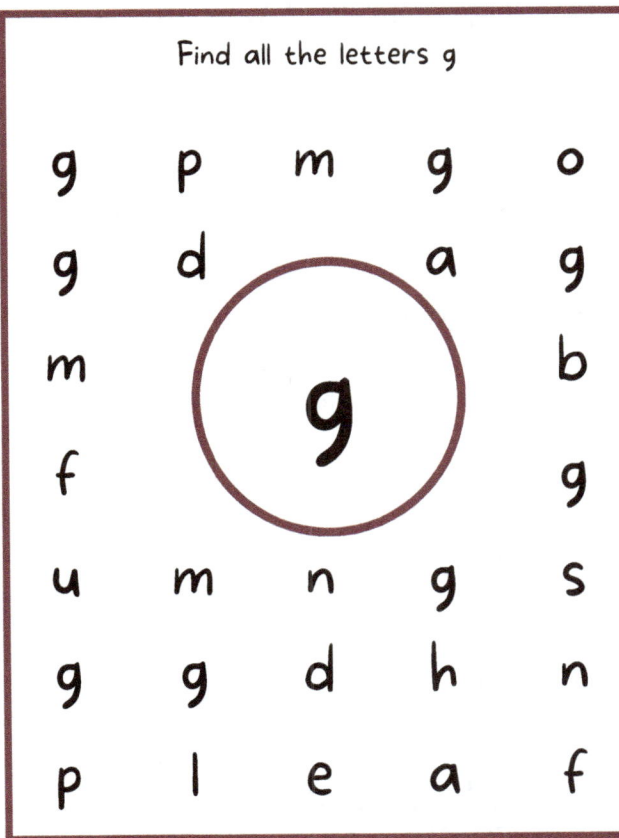

Find all the letters g

g p m g o

g d   a g

m   g   b

f   g

u m n g s

g g d h n

p l e a f

Psalm 71:22 (KJV)
22) I will also praise thee with the psaltery, even thy truth, O my God: unto thee will I sing with the harp, O thou Holy One of Israel.

Holy One

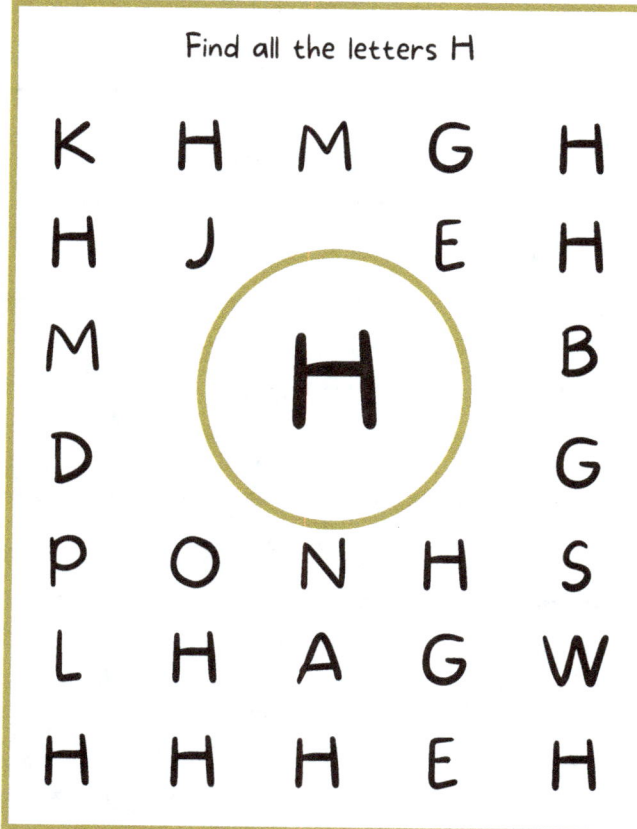

Find all the letters H

K	H	M	G	H
H	J		E	H
M		H		B
D				G
P	O	N	H	S
L	H	A	G	W
H	H	H	E	H

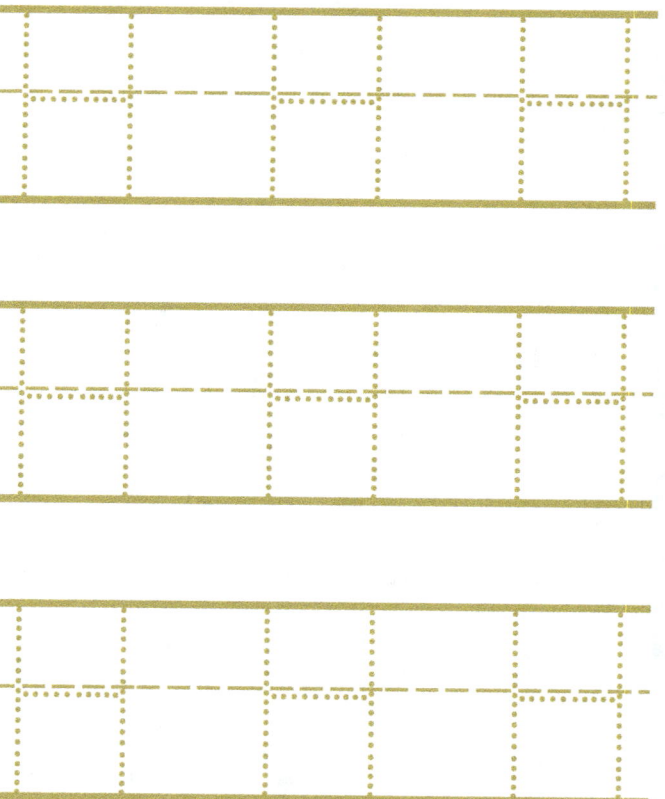

Colossians 1:18 (KJV)
18) And he is the head of the body, the church: who is the beginning, the firstborn from the dead; that in all things he might have the preeminence.

Head of the Church

Find all the letters h

h	e	j	h	s
o	h		f	p
m		h		h
h				g
f	h	n	h	h
h	a	h	r	y
w	e	t	h	v

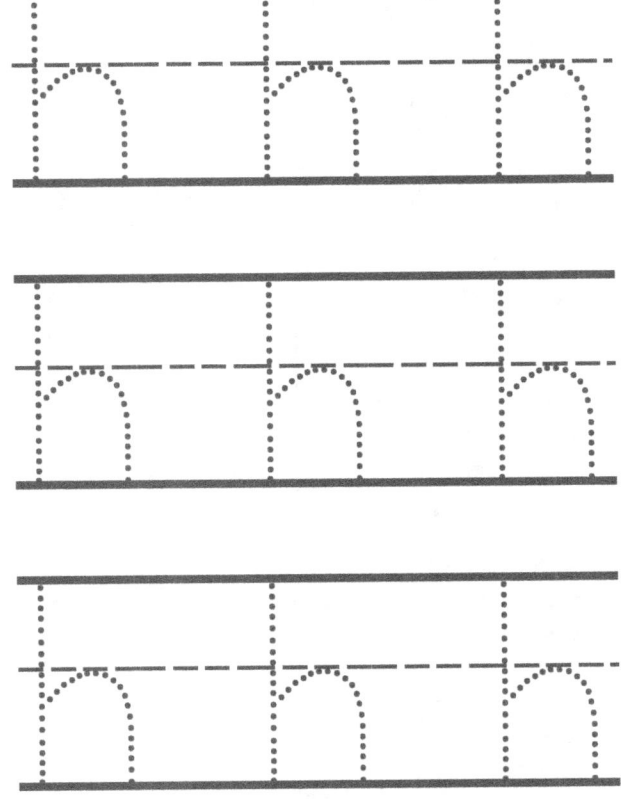

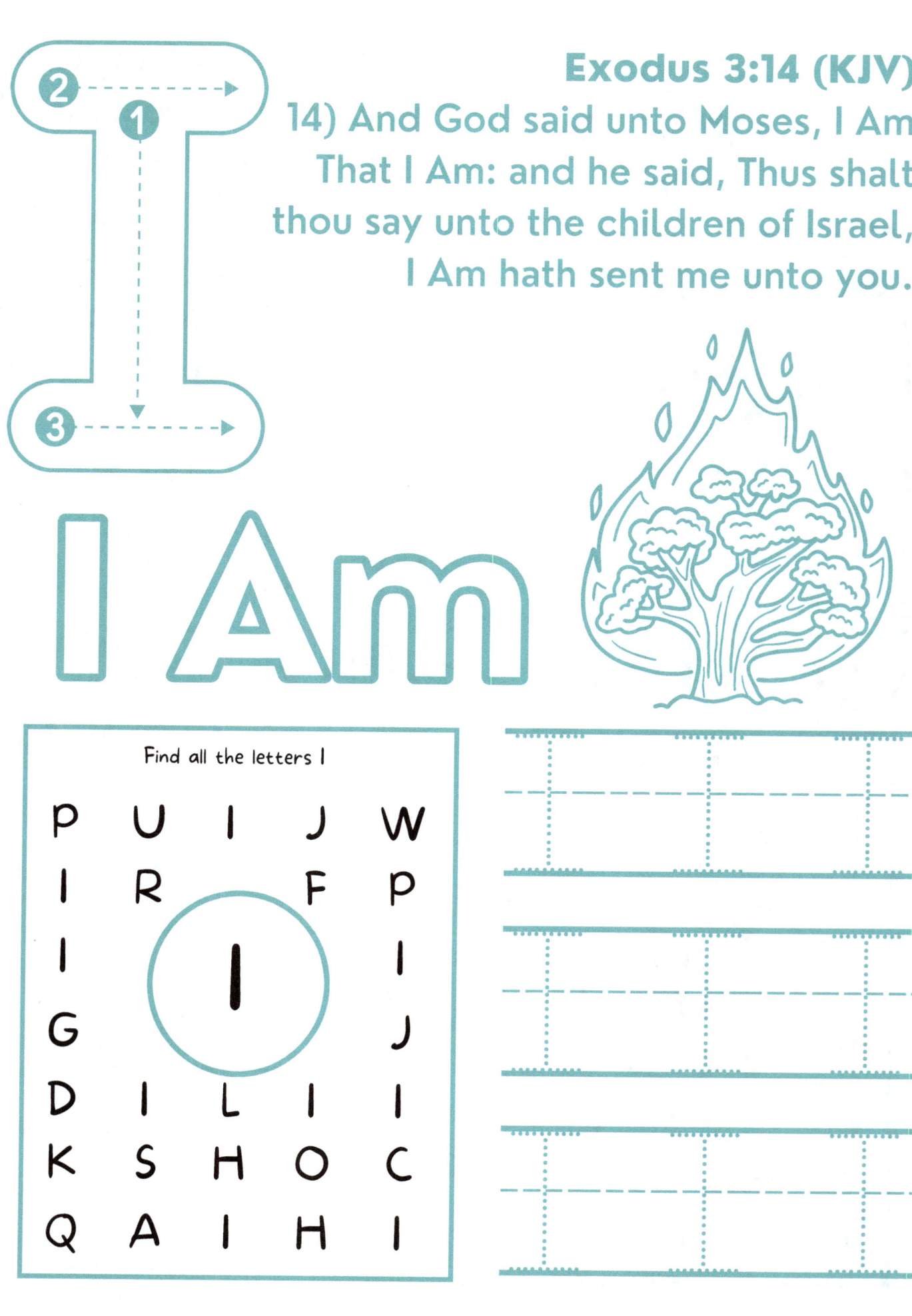

Exodus 3:14 (KJV)

14) And God said unto Moses, I Am That I Am: and he said, Thus shalt thou say unto the children of Israel, I Am hath sent me unto you.

I Am

Find all the letters I

P	U	I	J	W
I	R		F	P
I		I		P
G				J
D	I	L	I	J
K	S	H	O	C
Q	A	I	H	I

Mathew 1:23 (KJV)

23) Behold, a virgin shall be with child, and shall bring forth a son, and they shall call his name Emmanuel, which being interpreted is, God with us.

Immanuel

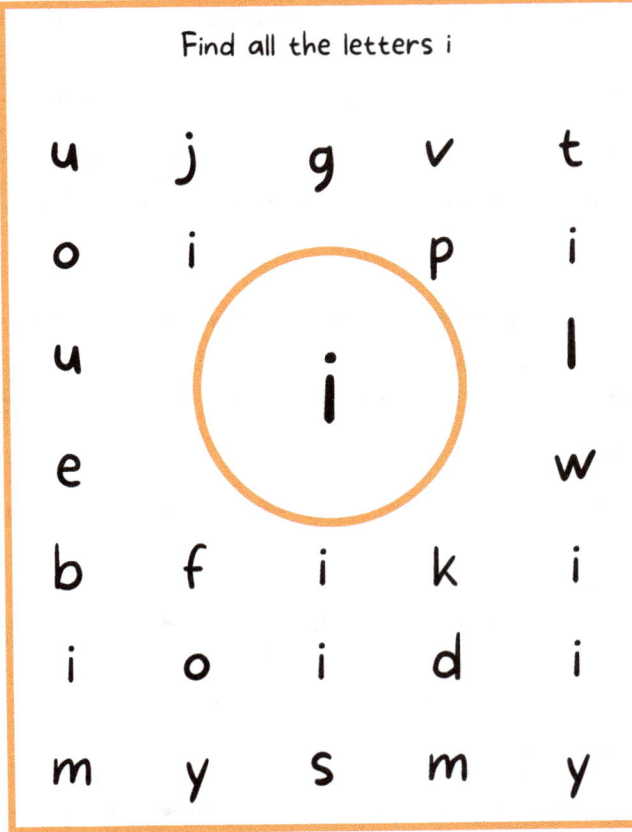

Find all the letters i

u	j	g	v	t
o	i		p	i
u		i		l
e				w
b	f	i	k	i
i	o	i	d	i
m	y	s	m	y

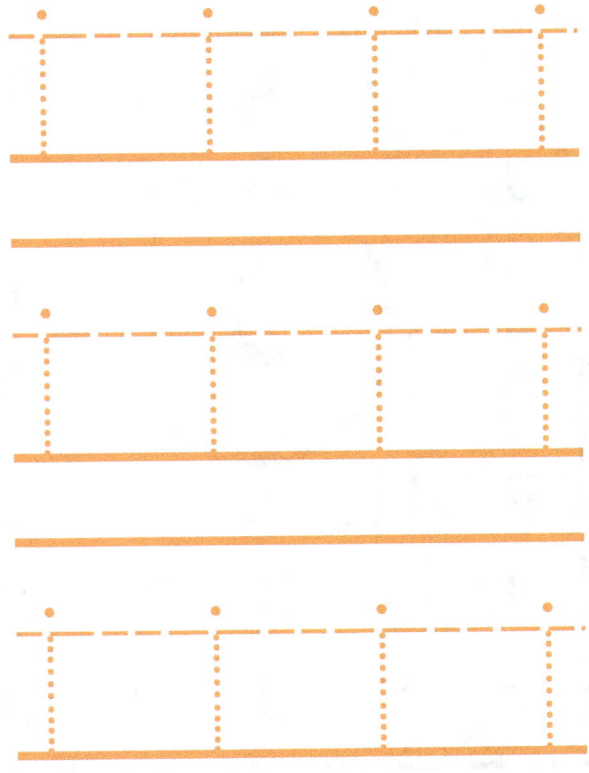

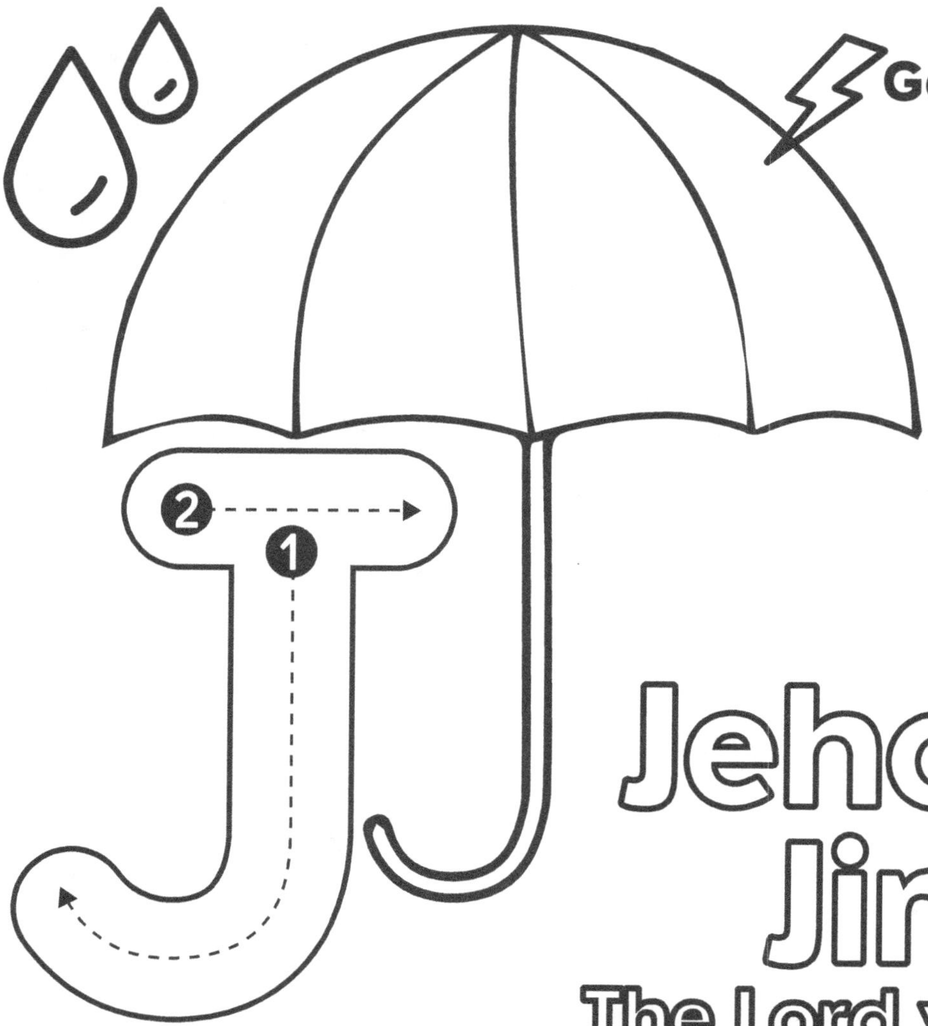

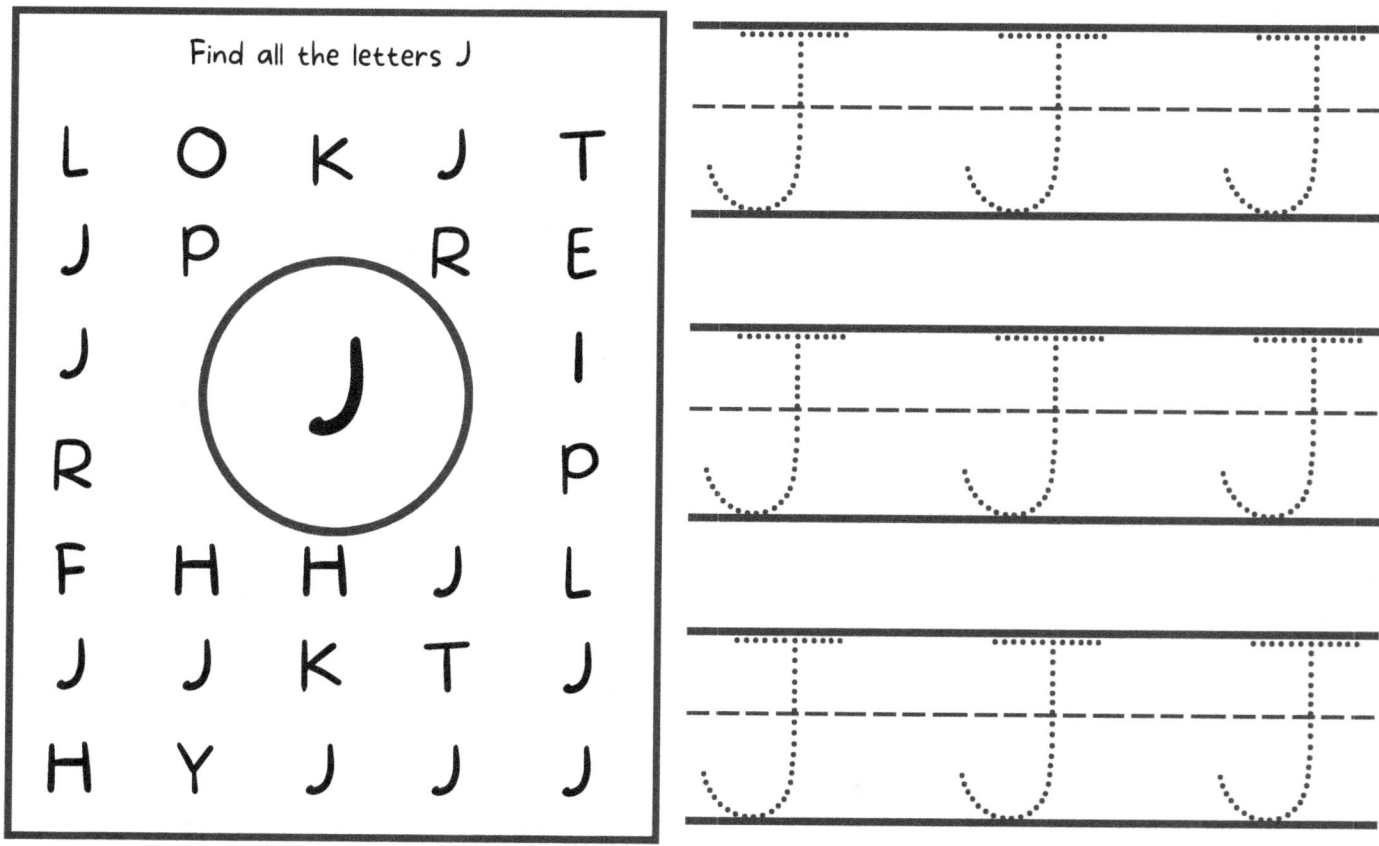

Genesis 22:14 (KJV)

14) And Abraham called the name of that place Jehovahjireh: as it is said to this day, In the mount of the Lord it shall be seen.

Jehovah-Jireh
The Lord will Provide

Find all the letters J

L	O	K	J	T
J	P	R	T	E
J		J		I
R				P
F	H	H	J	L
J	J	K	T	J
H	Y	J	J	J

Titus 3:5–7 (KJV)

5) Not by works of righteousness which we have done, but according to his mercy he saved us, by the washing of regeneration, and renewing of the Holy Ghost; 6) Which he shed on us abundantly through Jesus Christ our Saviour; 7) That being justified by his grace, we should be made heirs according to the hope of eternal life.

Jesus Christ our Savior

Find all the letters j

j	y	c	h	n
o	a		j	g
p		**j**		x
j				j
j	d	i	i	w
k	r	k	e	t
f	i	j	u	j

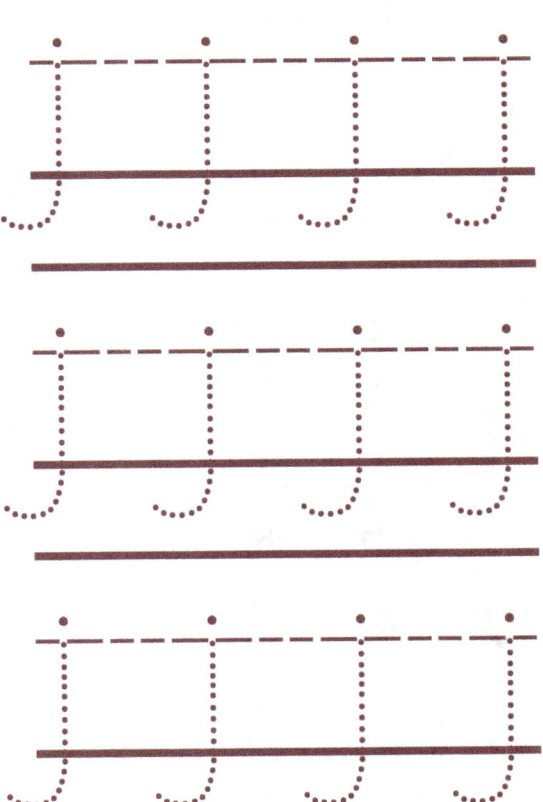

Revelation 19:16 (KJV)

16) And he hath on his vesture and on his thigh a name written, King Of Kings, And Lord Of Lords.

King of Kings and Lord Of Lords

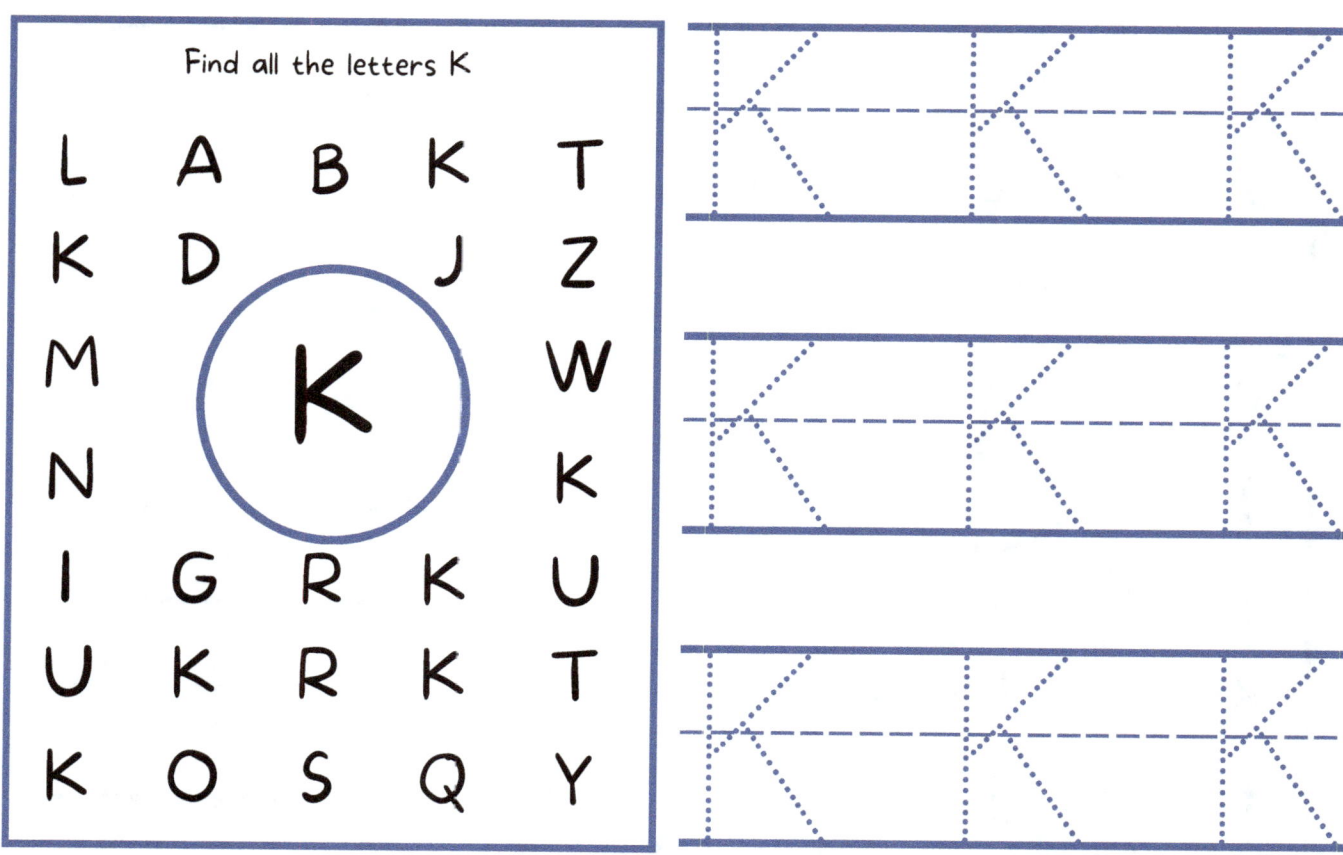

Find all the letters K

L	A	B	K	T
K	D		J	Z
M		K		W
N				K
I	G	R	K	U
U	K	R	K	T
K	O	S	Q	Y

Psalm 121:5 (KJV)

5) The Lord is thy keeper: the Lord is thy shade upon thy right hand.

keeper

Find all the letters k

k	e	c	q	t
k	k		y	k
o		k		k
g				b
n	w	k	a	z
j	k	q	u	k
d	k	l	k	s

John 1:29 (KJV)

29) The next day John seeth Jesus coming unto him, and saith, Behold the Lamb of God, which taketh away the sin of the world.

Lamb of God

Find all the letters L

P O A L K
L R Y L
K L G
G A
L E M B K
L O Q S L
W R L L C

Light of the World

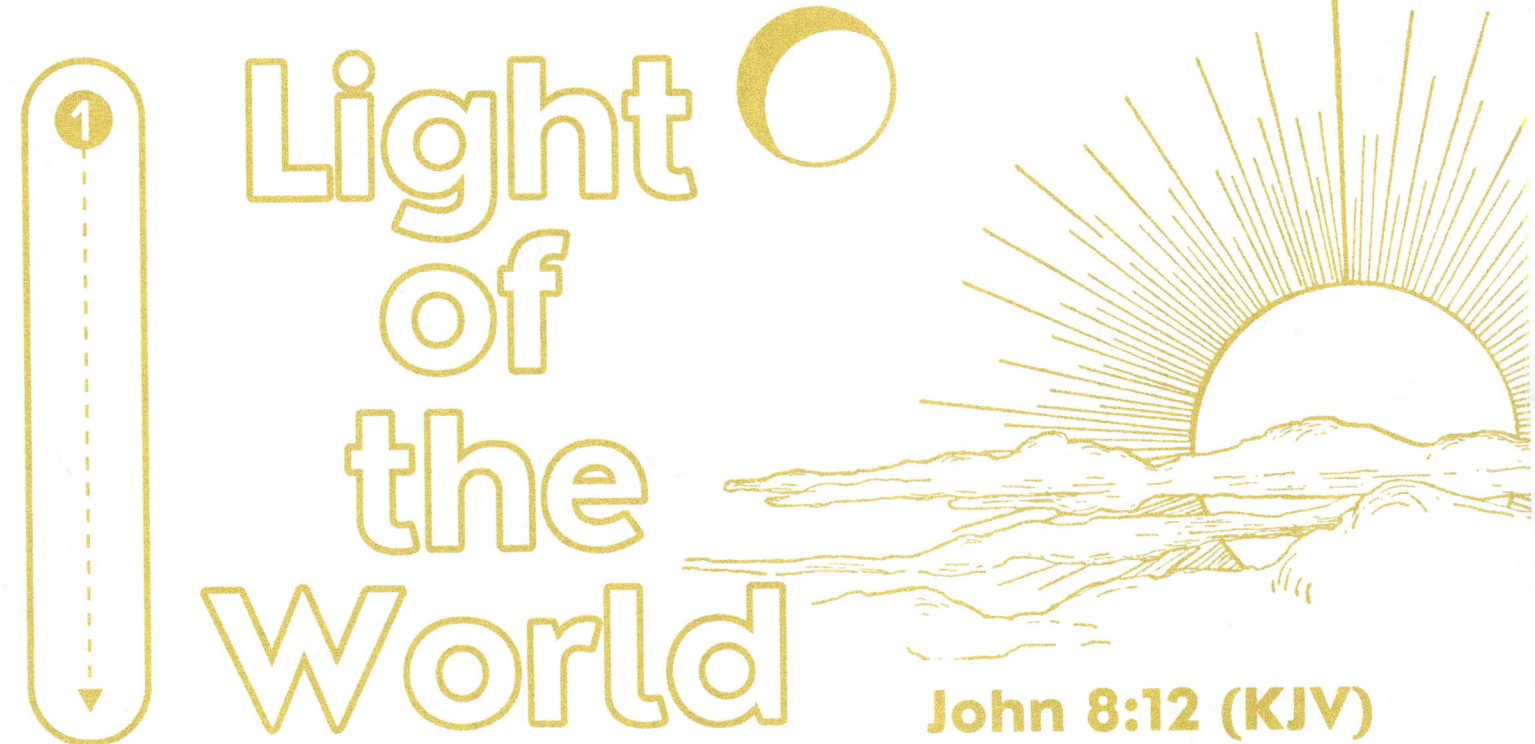

John 8:12 (KJV)

12) Then spake Jesus again unto them, saying, I am the light of the world: he that followeth me shall not walk in darkness, but shall have the light of life.

Find all the letters l

k	l	n	q	l
s	b		i	j
r		l		u
l				e
a	l	t	c	l
t	p	a	l	v
q	l	e	f	m

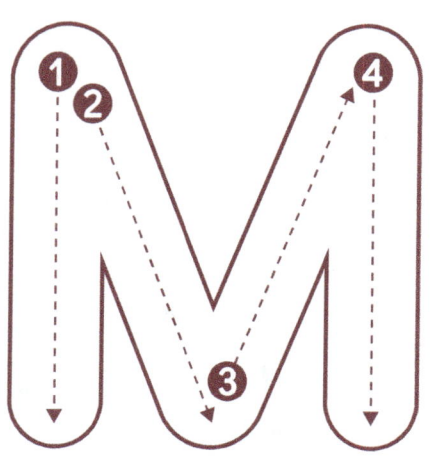

John 4:25-26 (KJV)

25) The woman saith unto him, I know that Messias cometh, which is called Christ: when he is come, he will tell us all things. 26) Jesus saith unto her, I that speak unto thee am he.

Messiah

Find all the letters M

F	T	Q	M	A
S	M		S	A
H		M		O
B				C
M	J	L	N	P
Q	M	A	I	X
M	K	B	M	M

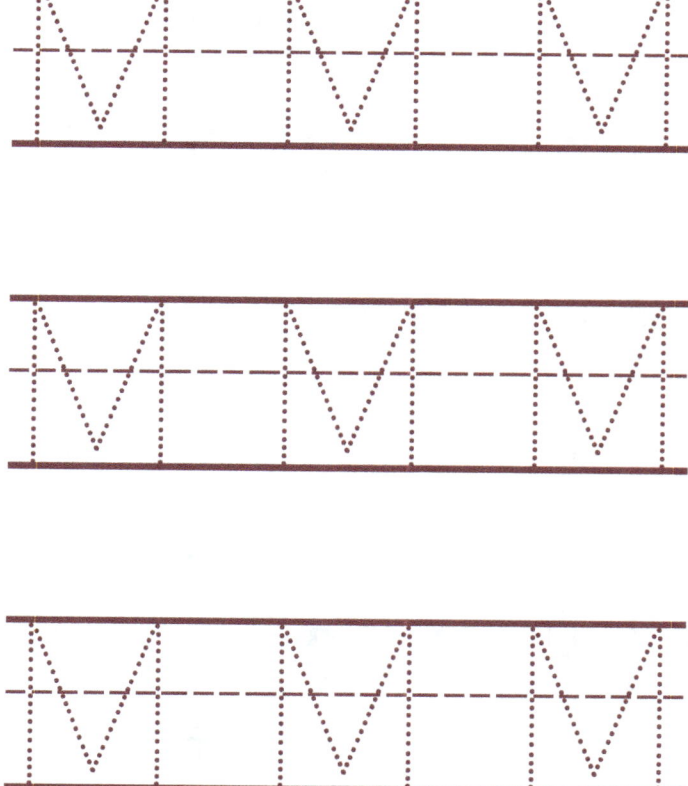

Psalm 145:8-9 (KJV)
8) The Lord is gracious, and full of compassion; slow to anger, and of great mercy.
9) The Lord is good to all: and his tender mercies are over all his works.

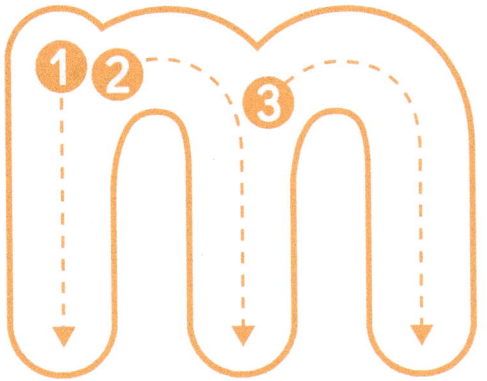

Merciful

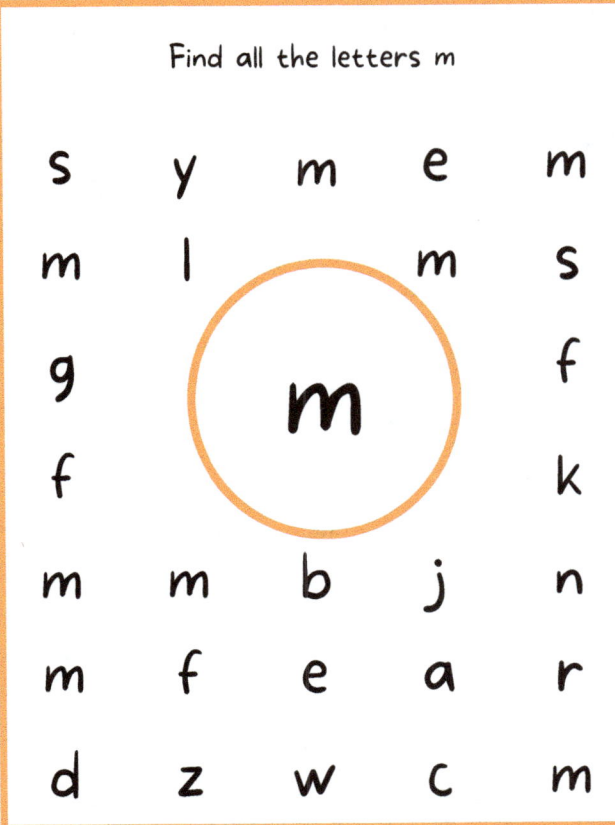

Find all the letters m

s	y	m	e	m
m	l		m	s
g		m		f
f				k
m	m	b	j	n
m	f	e	a	r
d	z	w	c	m

HELLO
MY NAME IS

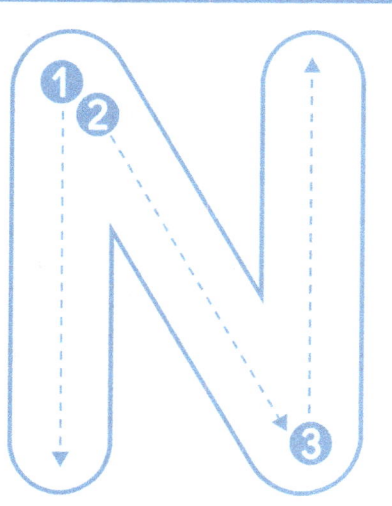

Philippians 2:9-10 (KJV)
9) Wherefore God also hath highly exalted him, and given him a name which is above every name: 10) That at the name of Jesus every knee should bow, of things in heaven, and things in earth, and things under the earth;

Name that is above every name

Find all the letters N

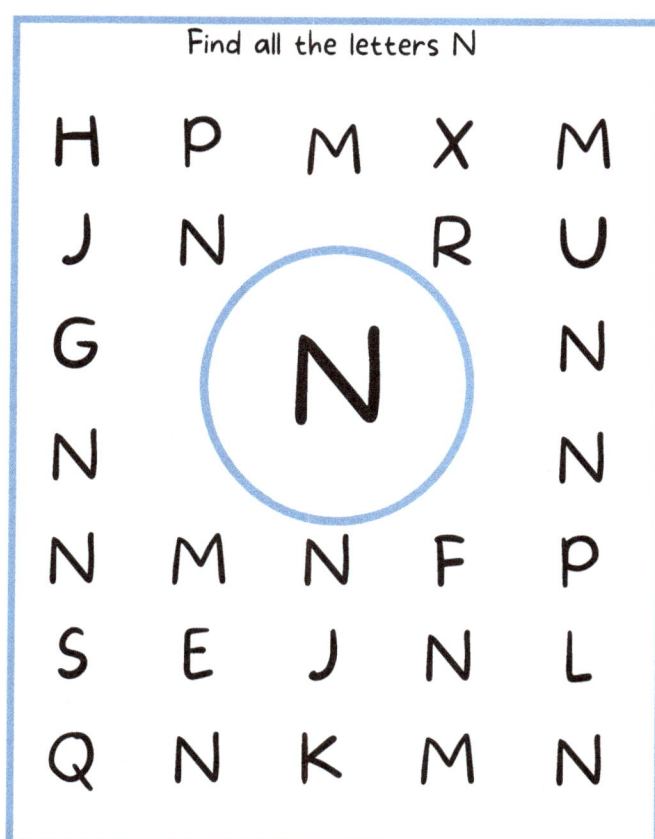

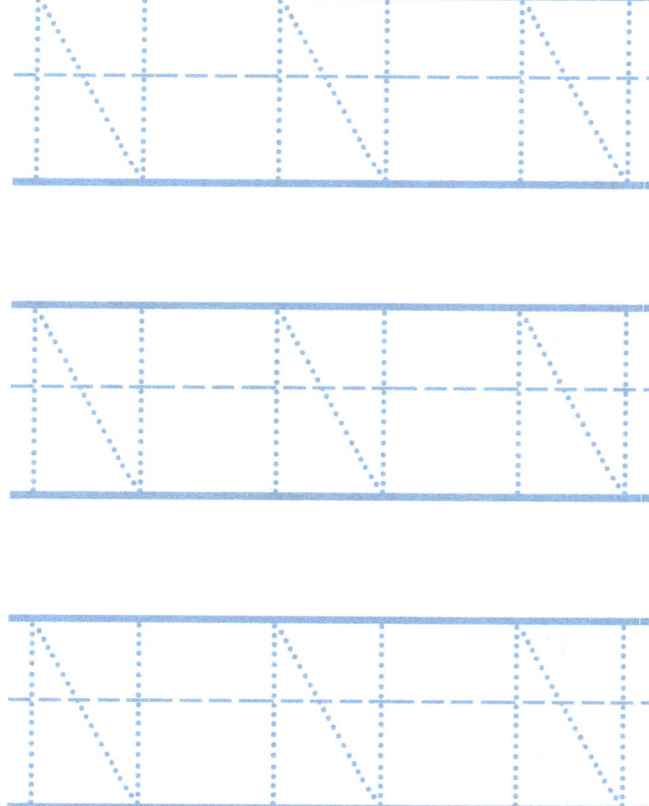

Matthew 2:23 (KJV)
23) And he came and dwelt in a city called Nazareth: that it might be fulfilled which was spoken by the prophets, He shall be called a Nazarene.

Nazarene

Find all the letters n

l	n	k	z	n
n	u		b	n
f		n		g
d				n
e	t	l	n	r
q	n	n	w	s
n	y	n	o	q

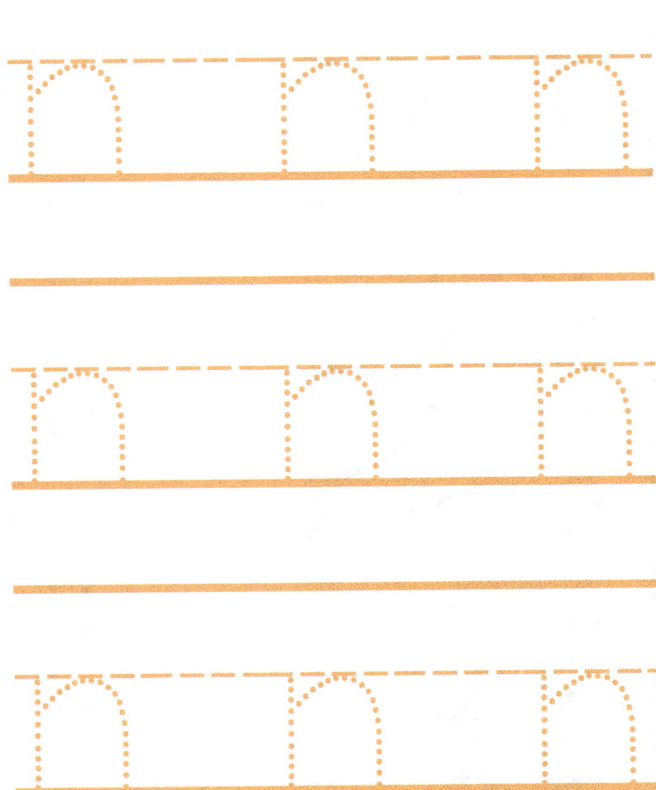

1 Timothy 1:17 (KJV)

17) Now unto the King eternal, immortal, invisible, the only wise God, be honour and glory for ever and ever. Amen.

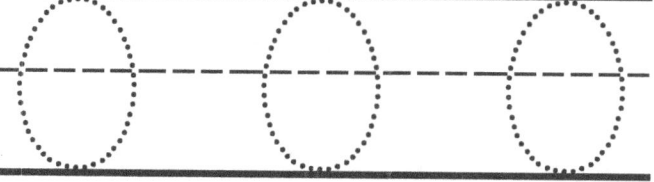

THE ONE TRUE GOD

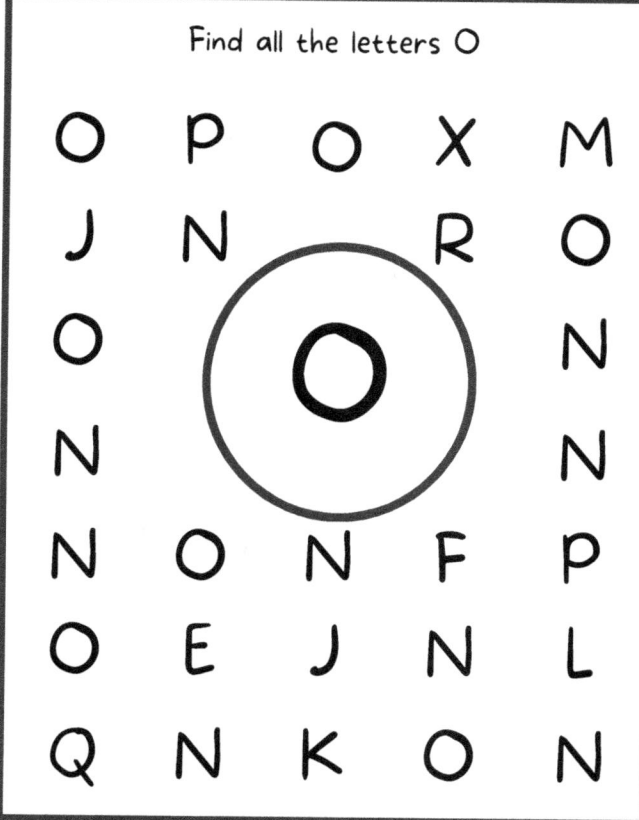

Find all the letters O

O	P	O	X	M
J	N		R	O
O		O		M
N				N
N	O	N	F	P
O	E	J	N	L
Q	N	K	O	N

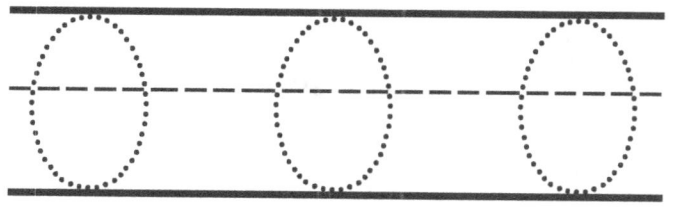

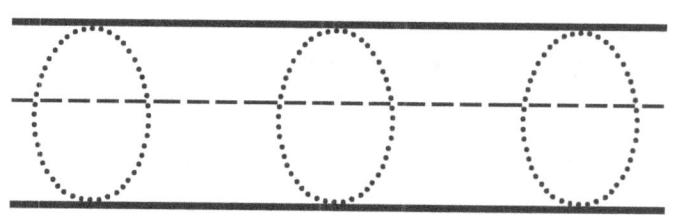

Revelation 19:6 (KJV)

6) And I heard as it were the voice of a great multitude, and as the voice of many waters, and as the voice of mighty thunderings, saying, Alleluia: for the Lord God omnipotent reigneth.

Omnipotent
(having unlimited power)

Find all the letters o

l	o	q	s	m
p	d		u	c
g				a
o		o		s
h	b	o	l	h
k	w	y	d	o
o	o	o	d	i

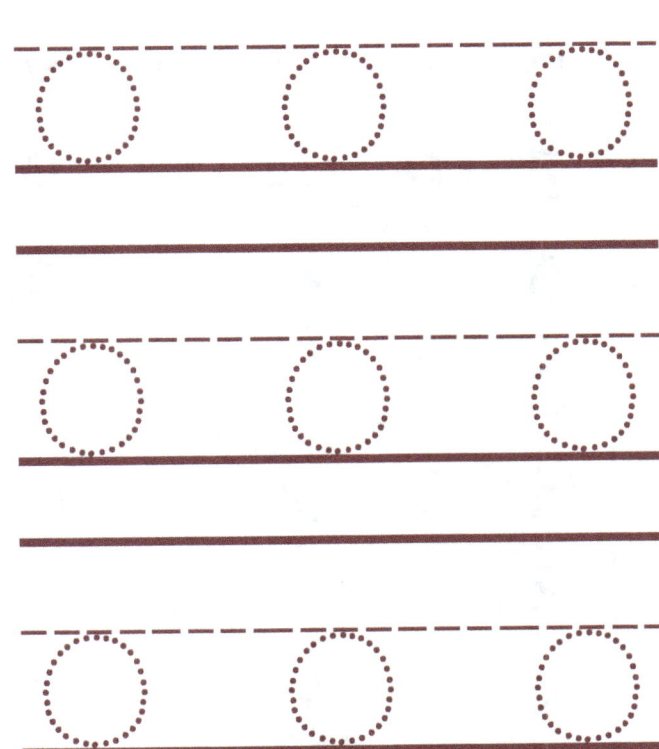

Psalm 46:1 (KJV)
1) God is our refuge and strength, a very present help in trouble.

Present Help in Trouble

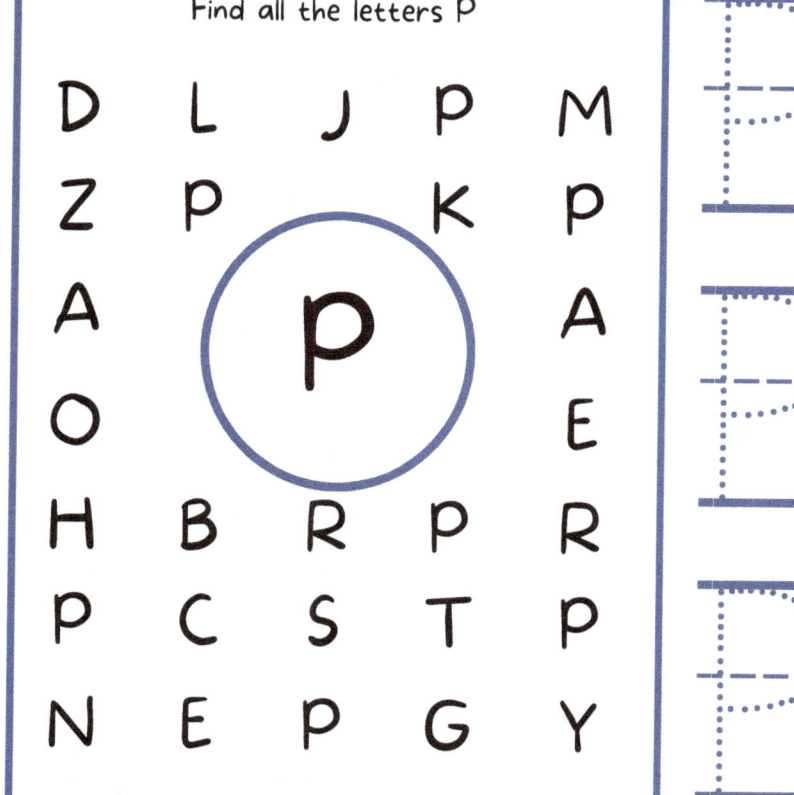

Find all the letters P

D	L	J	P	M
Z	P		K	M
A		P		A
O				E
H	B	R	P	R
P	C	S	T	P
N	E	P	G	Y

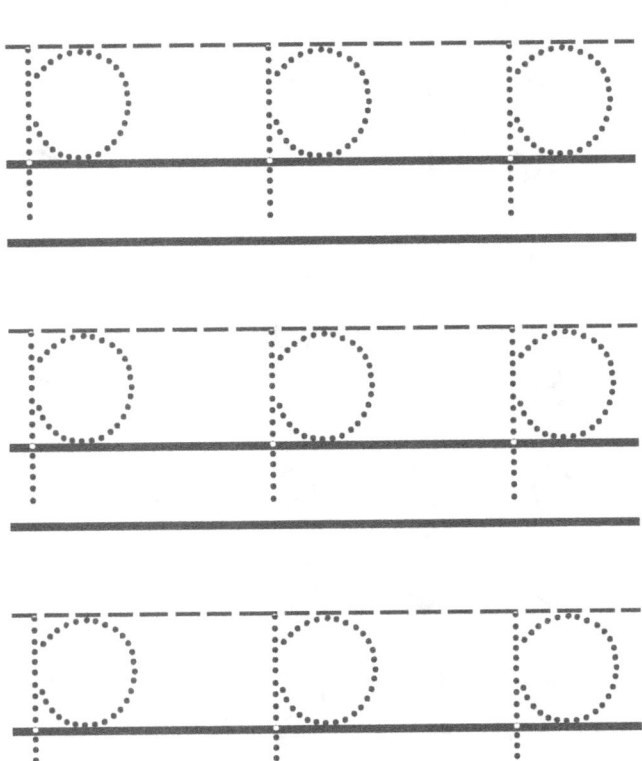

Isaiah 9:6 (KJV)

6) For unto us a child is born, unto us a son is given: and the government shall be upon his shoulder: and his name shall be called Wonderful, Counsellor, The mighty God, The everlasting Father, The Prince of Peace.

Peace

Prince of Peace

Find all the letters p

r	p	j	s	p
p	k		n	p
e		p		a
p				p
l	o	f	d	g
m	p	x	p	h
p	c	q	p	v

Psalm 107:29-30 (KJV)

29) He maketh the storm a calm, so that the waves thereof are still.
30) Then are they glad because they be quiet; so he bringeth them unto their desired haven.

Quieter of Storms

Find all the letters Q

D	Q	N	Q	E
W	L		M	G
Q		Q		P
S				K
Q	F	R	Q	A
O	Q	C	L	Q
E	P	Q	H	X

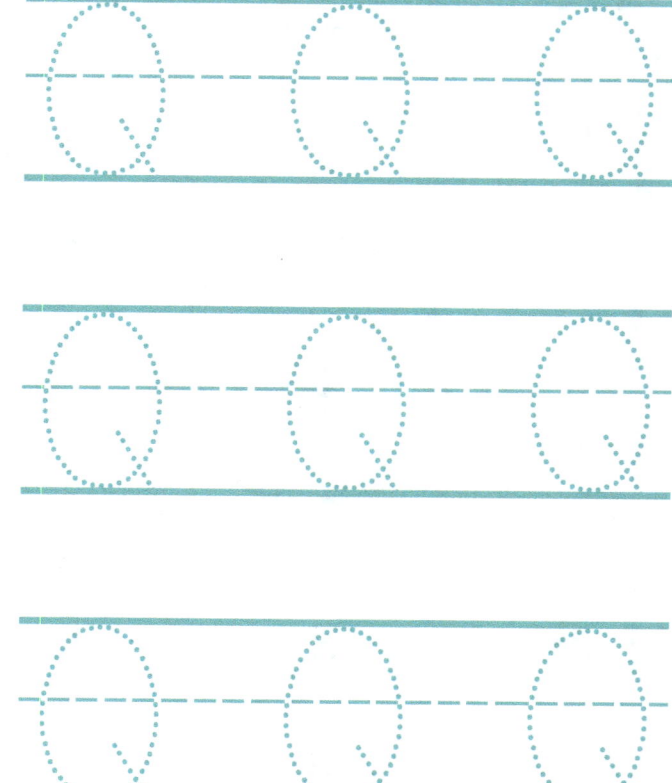

Exodus 20:5 (KJV)

5) Thou shalt not bow down thyself to them, nor serve them: for I the Lord thy God am a jealous God, visiting the iniquity of the fathers upon the children unto the third and fourth generation of them that hate me;

Qanna' `El
(Jealous God)

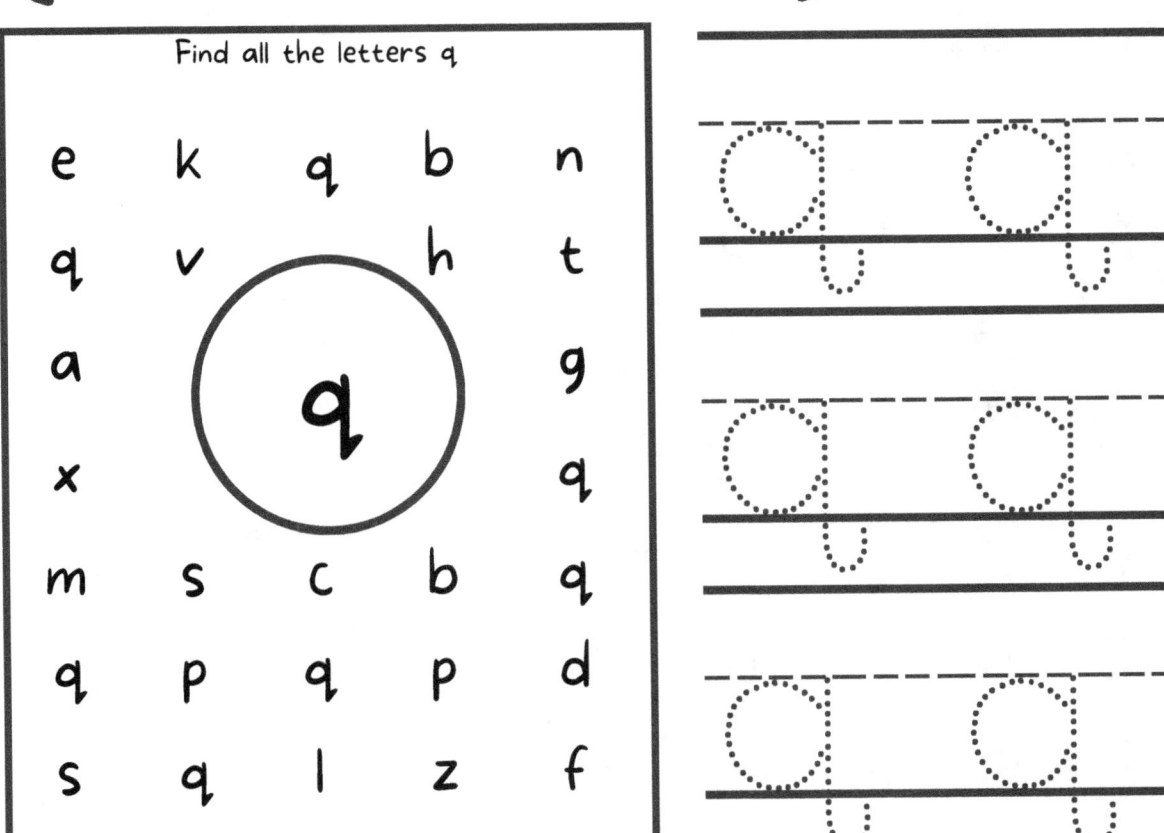

Find all the letters q

e	k	q	b	n
q	v		h	t
a				g
x		q		q
m	s	c	b	q
q	p	q	p	d
s	q	l	z	f

John 11:25 (KJV)
25) Jesus said unto her, I am the resurrection, and the life: he that believeth in me, though he were dead, yet shall he live:

The Resurrection and The Life

Find all the letters R

L	R	V	N	T
P	E		K	T
Y		R		G
G				W
H	Y	R	U	C
R	R	D	X	B
T	F	K	R	M

Psalm 90:1 (KJV)

1) Lord, thou hast been our dwelling place in all generations.

Refuge

Find all the letters r

r	e	r	r	n
c	b		p	e
g		r		b
r				f
j	r	k	l	z
v	f	g	d	h
w	r	m	o	k

S — Son of God

Luke 1:35 (KJV)

35) And the angel answered and said unto her, The Holy Ghost shall come upon thee, and the power of the Highest shall overshadow thee: therefore also that holy thing which shall be born of thee shall be called the Son of God.

Find all the letters S

E	A	S	V	S
S	E		X	O
S		S		N
B				S
G	L	W	S	Q
S	K	F	M	Y
S	D	S	R	T

Savior of the World

John 4:42 (KJV)

42) And said unto the woman, Now we believe, not because of thy saying: for we have heard him ourselves, and know that this is indeed the Christ, the Saviour of the world.

Find all the letters s

d	s	y	d	r
f	x		v	s
s		**S**		p
w				o
q	c	m	n	j
o	s	g	s	t
s	x	e	r	s

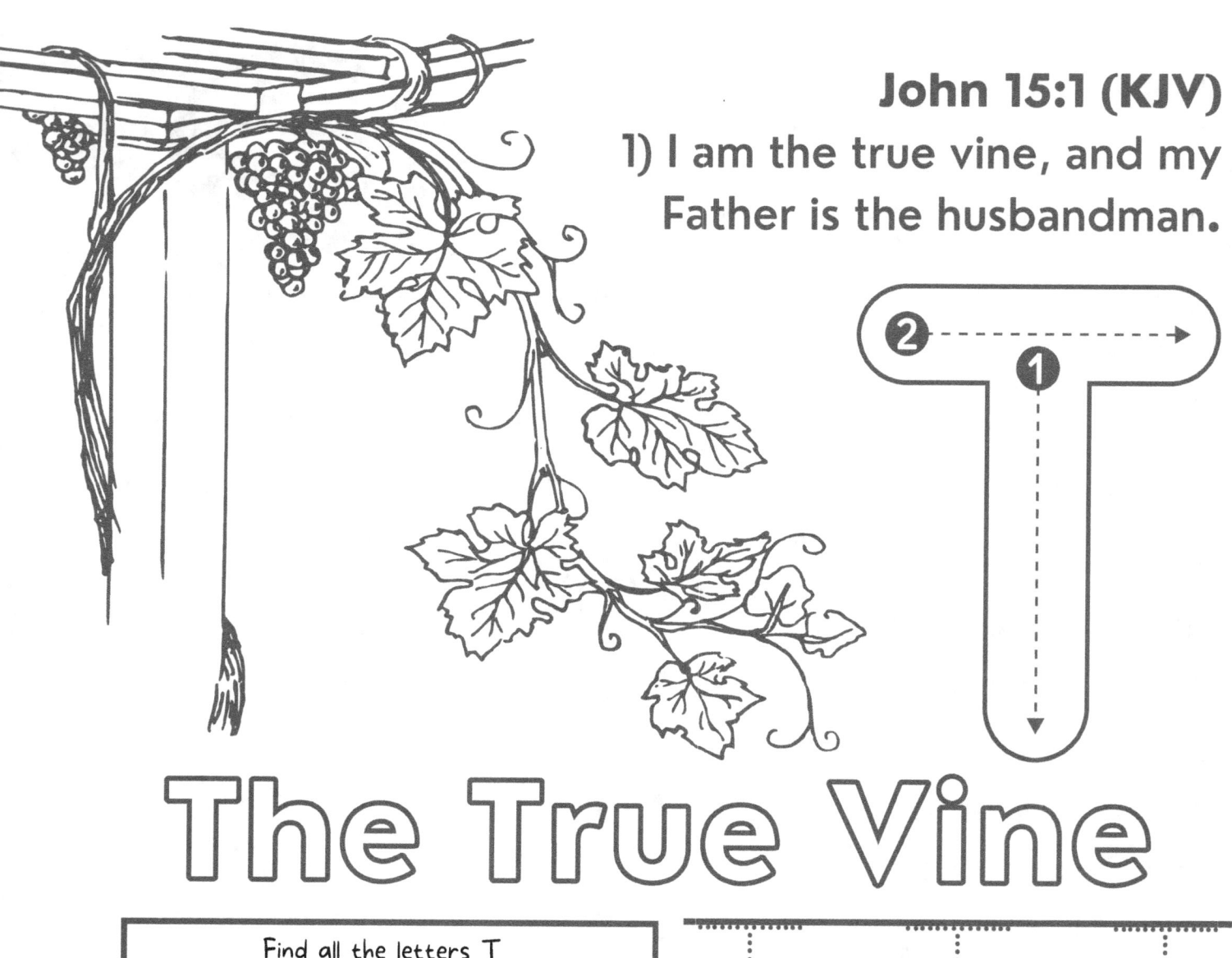

John 15:1 (KJV)

1) I am the true vine, and my Father is the husbandman.

The True Vine

Find all the letters T

H	C	D	L	T
F	T		G	T
B		T		T
C				J
S	T	N	H	I
X	T	O	K	T
L	Q	T	T	P
				V

John 14:6 (KJV)

6) Jesus saith unto him, I am the way, the truth, and the life: no man cometh unto the Father, but by me.

The Truth

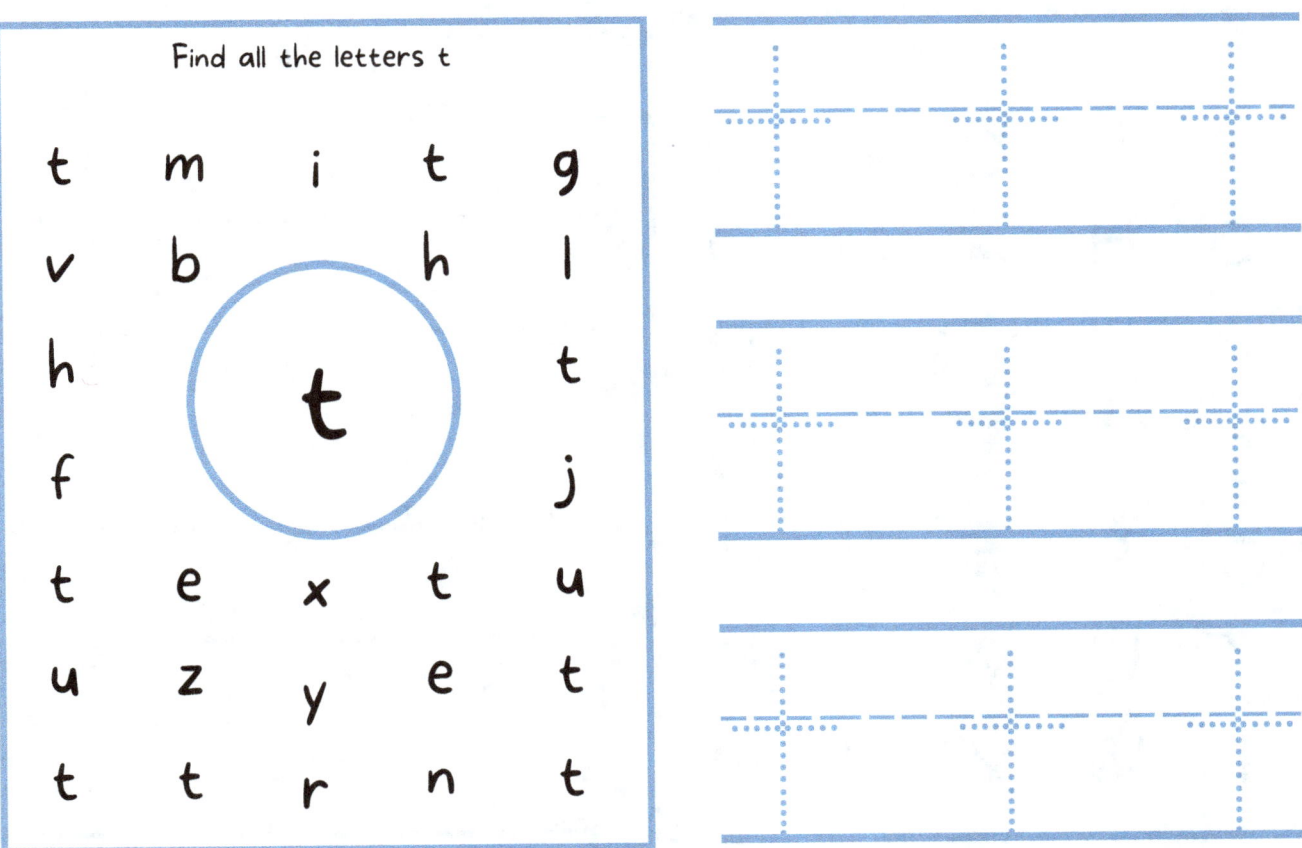

Find all the letters t

t	m	i	t	g
v	b		h	l
h		t		t
f				j
t	e	x	t	u
u	z	y	e	t
t	t	r	n	t

Psalm 59:10 (KJV)

10) The God of my mercy shall prevent me: God shall let me see my desire upon mine enemies.

Unfailing Love

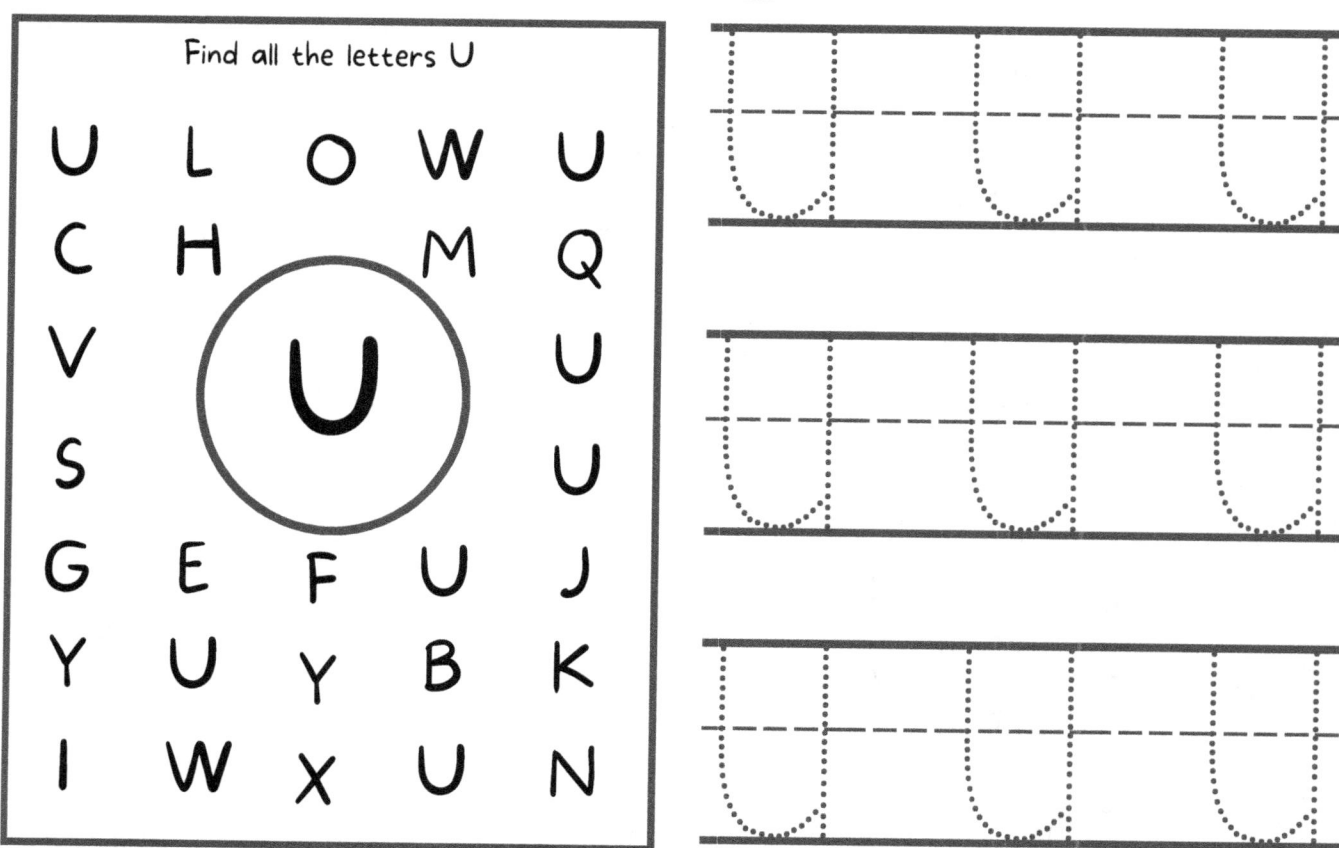

Find all the letters U

U	L	O	W	U
C	H			M	Q
V		U		U
S				U
G	E	F	U	J
Y	U	Y	B	K
I	W	X	U	N

The Uncorruptible God

Romans 1:23 (KJV)

23) And changed the glory of the uncorruptible God into an image made like to corruptible man, and to birds, and fourfooted beasts, and creeping things.

Find all the letters u

k	i	u	o	p
l	u		y	u
h		u		p
v				e
n	w	u	f	u
u	h	c	e	v
m	u	o	c	u

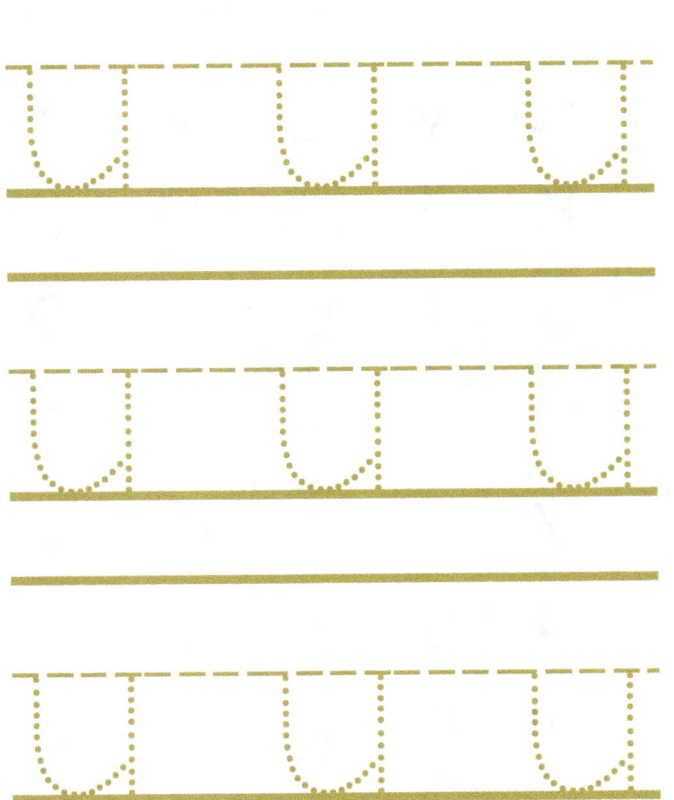

Very Present Help in Trouble

Psalm 46:1 (KJV)

1) God is our refuge and strength, a very present help in trouble.

Find all the letters V

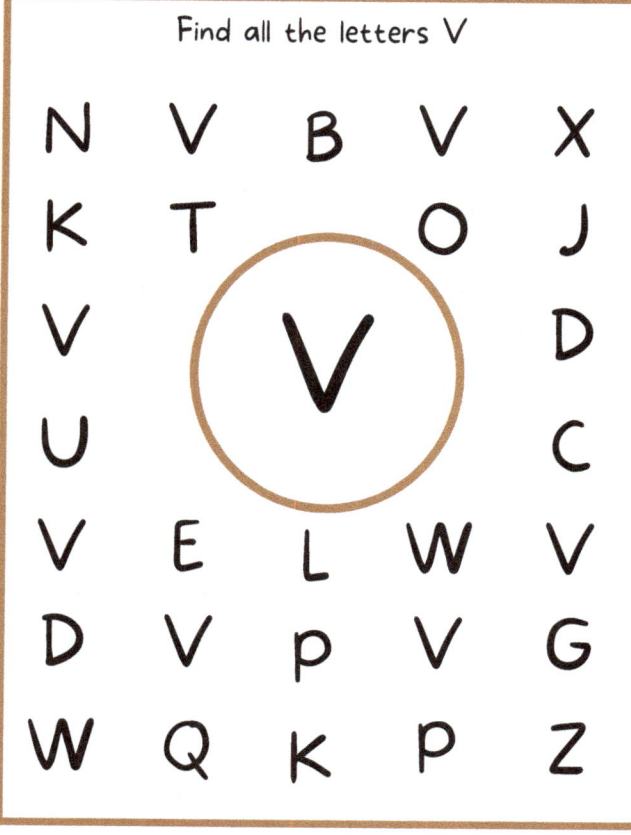

N	V	B	V	X
K	T		O	J
V		**V**		D
U				C
V	E	L	W	V
D	V	P	V	G
W	Q	K	P	Z

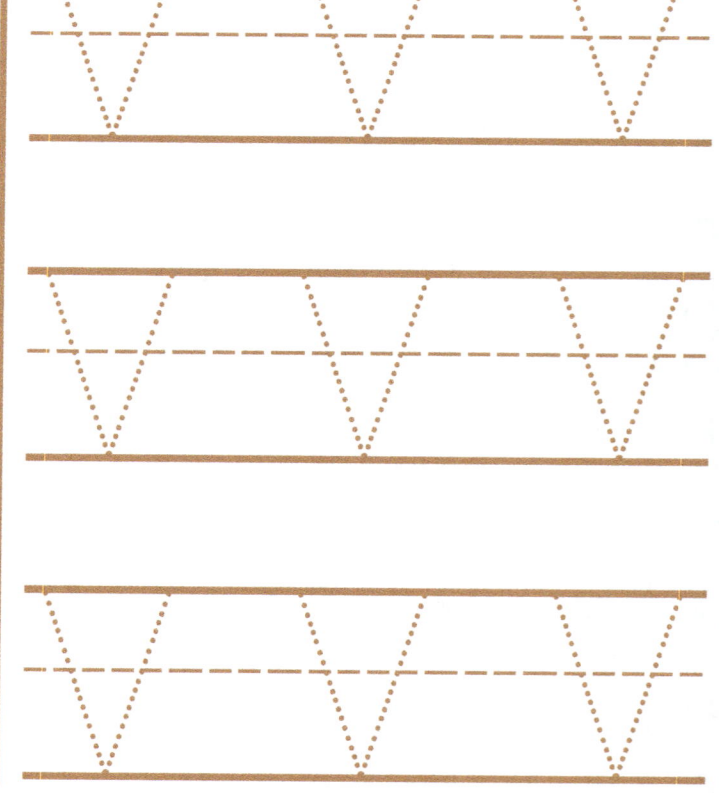

Victory

1 Cor.15:54 (KJV)
54) So when this corruptible shall have put on incorruption, and this mortal shall have put on immortality, then shall be brought to pass the saying that is written, Death is swallowed up in victory.

Find all the letters v

p	o	v	g	v
b	v		x	w
u		**v**		v
v				i
h	g	u	p	v
h	v	o	m	c
w	l	v	n	s

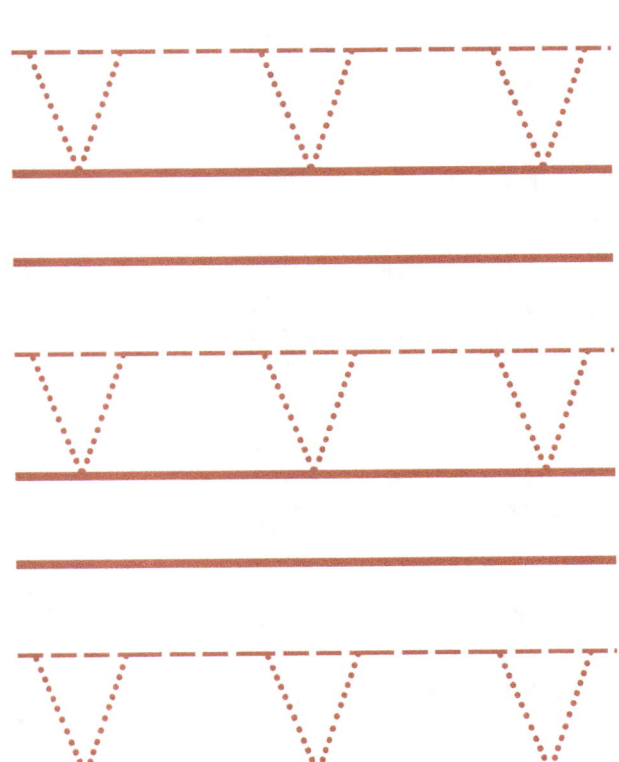

Wonderful Counselor

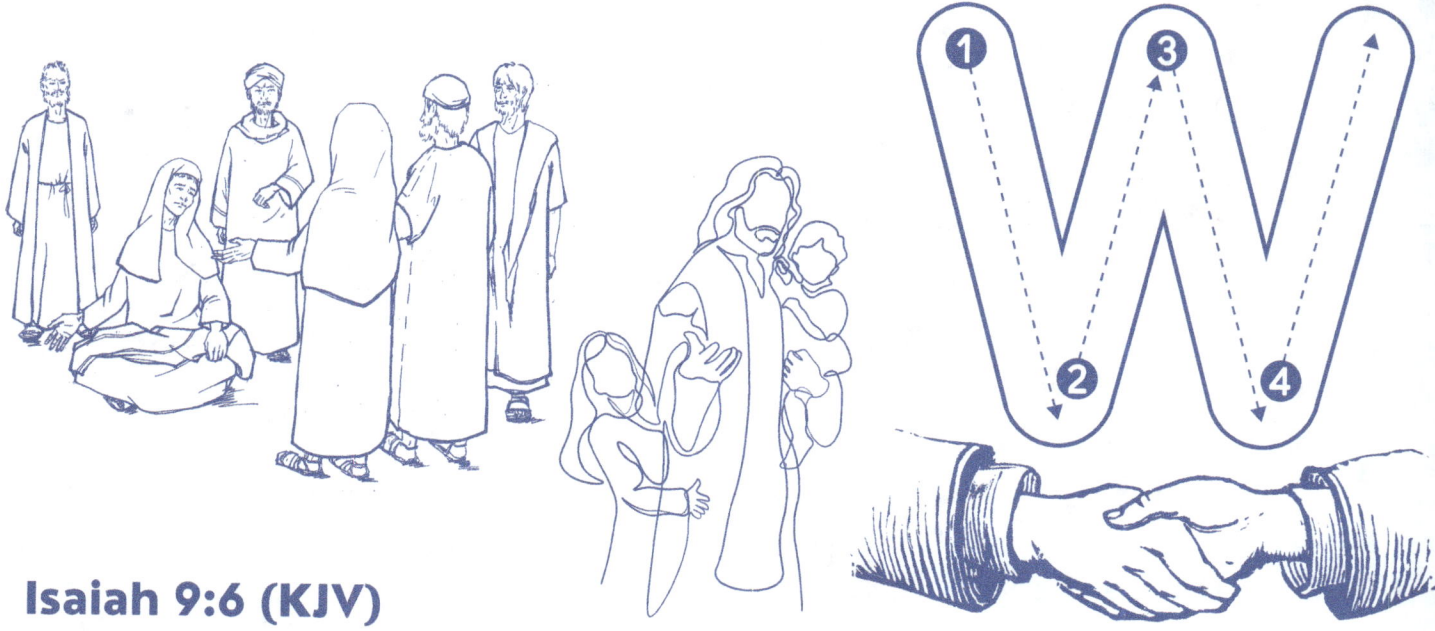

Isaiah 9:6 (KJV)

6) For unto us a child is born, unto us a son is given: and the government shall be upon his shoulder: and his name shall be called Wonderful, Counsellor, The mighty God, The everlasting Father, The Prince of Peace.

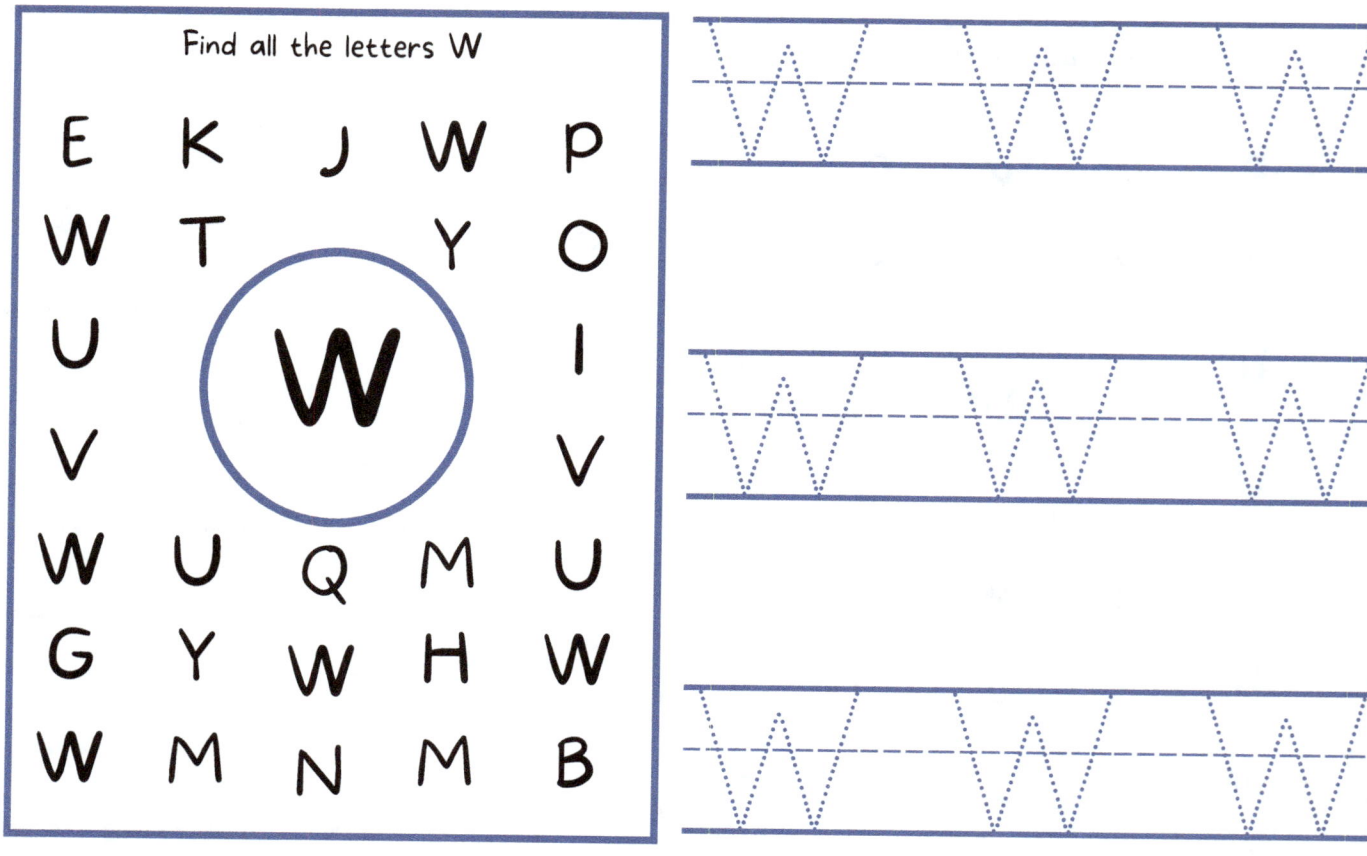

The Word of Life

I John 1:1 (KJV)

1) That which was from the beginning, which we have heard, which we have seen with our eyes, which we have looked upon, and our hands have handled, of the Word of life;

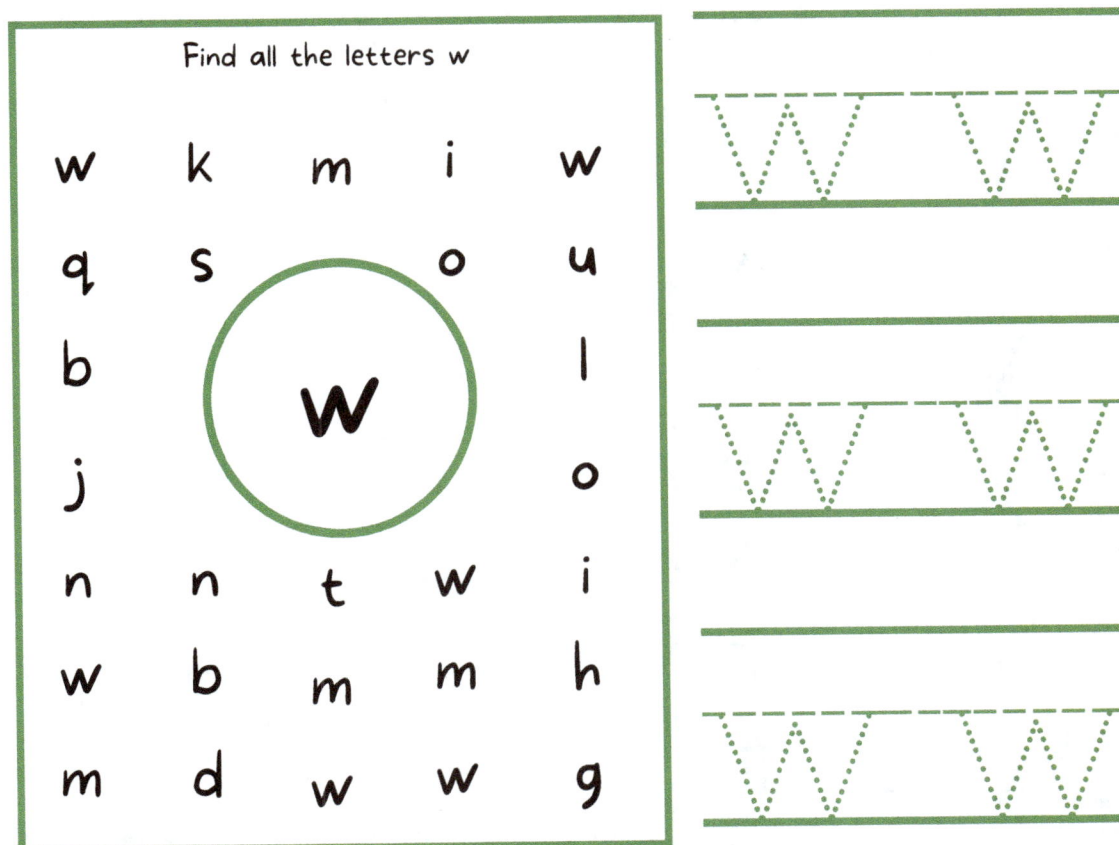

Find all the letters w

w	k	m	i	w
q	s		o	u
b		**W**		l
j				o
n	n	t	w	i
w	b	m	m	h
m	d	w	w	g

X Xristos (Greek for Christ)

Luke 23:35 (KJV)

35) And the people stood beholding. And the rulers also with them derided him, saying, He saved others; let him save himself, if he be Christ, the chosen of God.

Find all the letters X

EXcellent

Psalm 8:1 (KJV)
1) O Lord, our Lord, how excellent is thy name in all the earth! who hast set thy glory above the heavens.

Find all the letters x

g	o	x	t		r
v	p		o		k
x					l
u		**x**			x
h	l	w	n		x
x	u	f	x		k
w	x	j	c		z

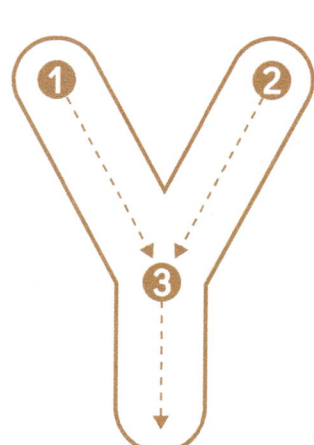

Y Yahweh
(Distinctly Proper Name for God)

Exodus 6:3 (KJV)

3) And I appeared unto Abraham, unto Isaac, and unto Jacob, by the name of God Almighty, but by my name Jehovah was I not known to them.

Find all the letters Y

P	T	R	H	Y
Y	Y		S	D
O		Y		Y
T				V
Y	G	U	N	Y
F	B	Y	W	Q
J	K	C	Y	X

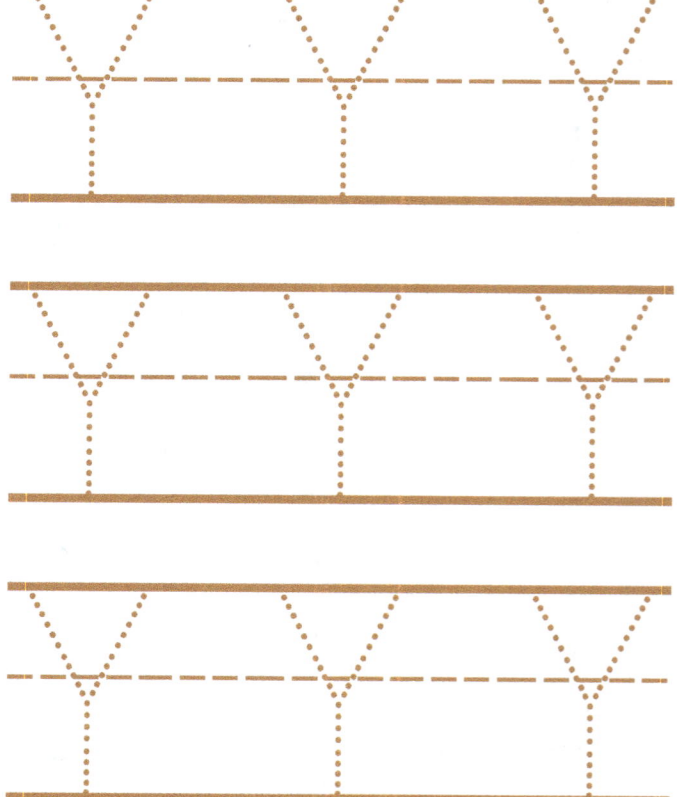

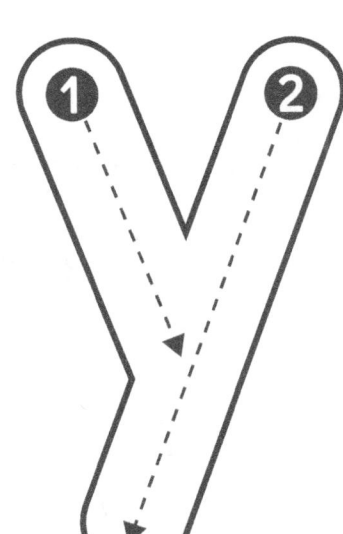

Y Yeshua

Name given to our Lord to denote His mission "to Save"

Matthew 1:21 (KJV)
21) And she shall bring forth a son, and thou shalt call his name Jesus: for he shall save his people from their sins.

Find all the letters y

k	p	y	y	b
u	u		j	r
y		**y**		h
i				y
g	l	p	f	z
y	y	w	q	y
y	o	m	y	e

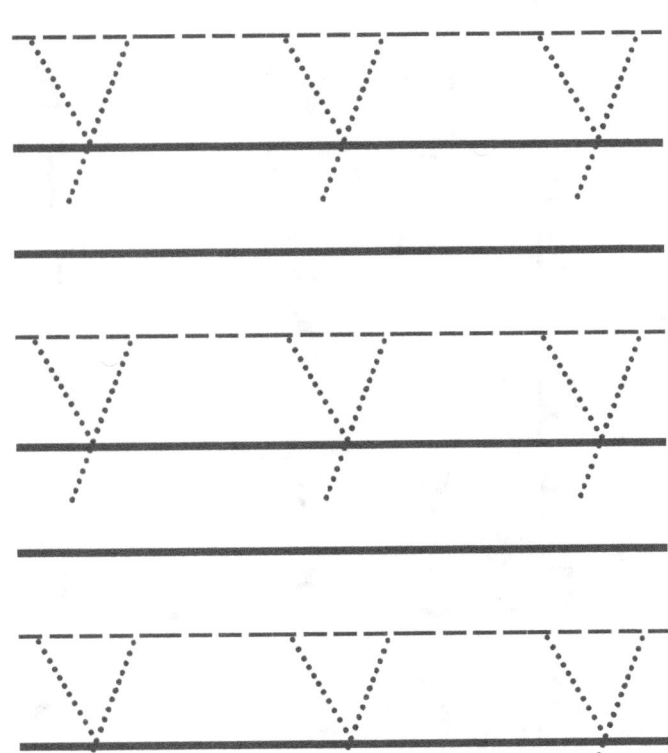

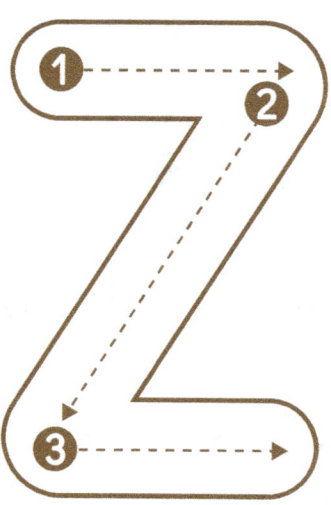

Z Zur (Hebrew for Rock)

1 Samuel 2:2 (KJV)
2) There is none holy as the Lord: for there is none beside thee: neither is there any rock like our God.

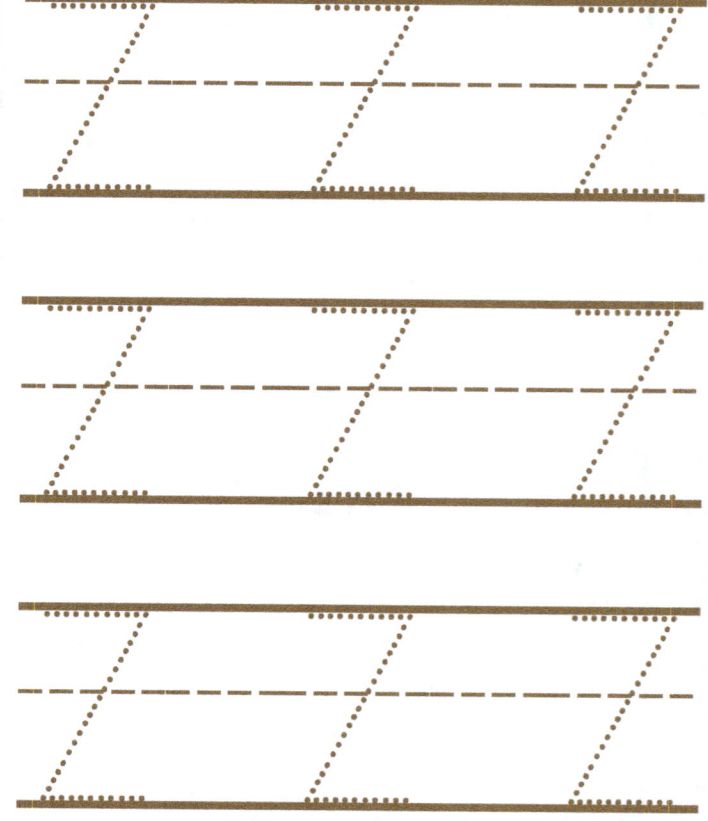

Find all the letters Z

L	M	W	Z	Z
Z	Z		S	I
X		Z		L
Q				O
H	Y	Z	Q	Z
F	B	G	Z	E
K	Z	D	R	A

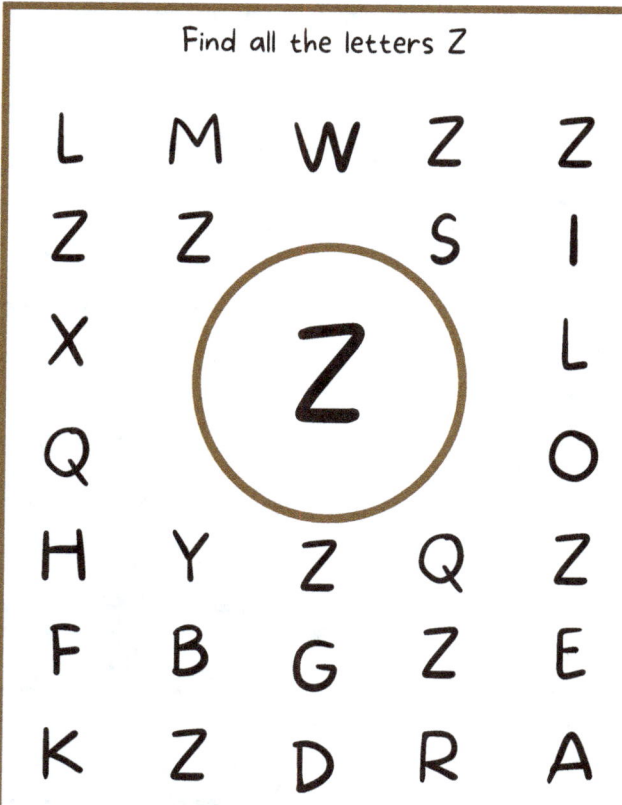

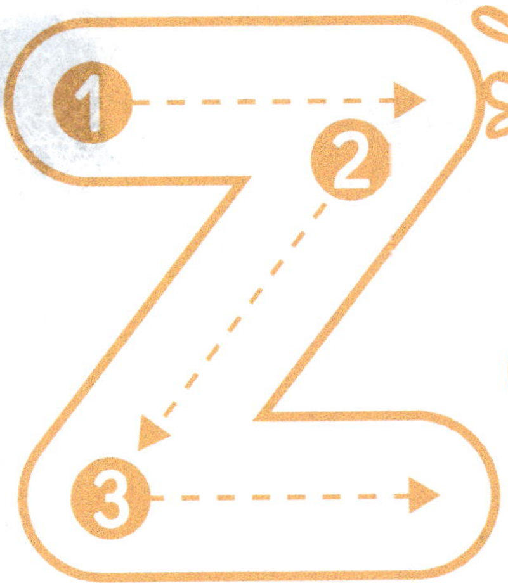

Z

John 2:17 (KJV)

17) And his disciples remembered that it was written, The zeal of thine house hath eaten me up.

Zeal of your House

Find all the letters z

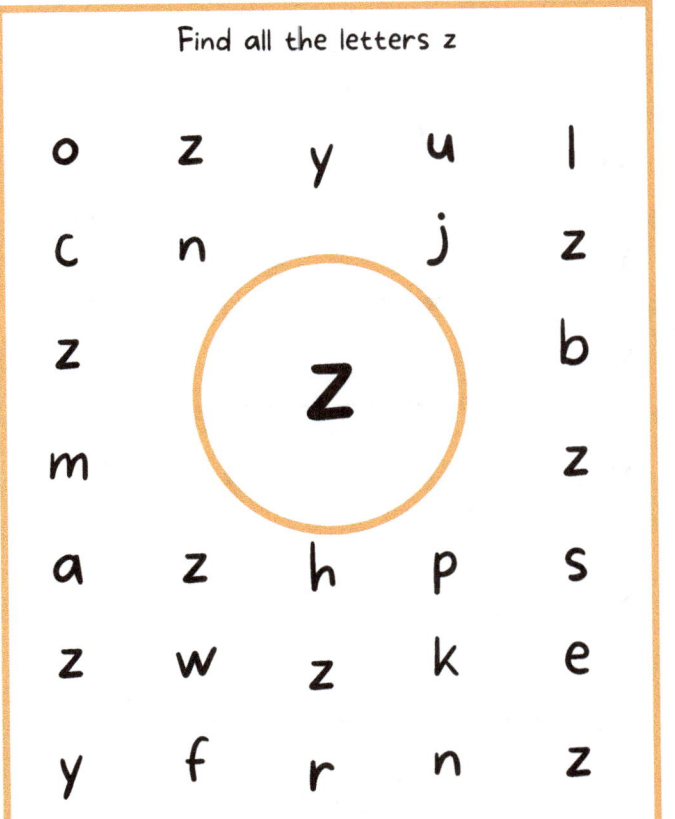

o	z	y	u	l
c	n		j	z
z		**Z**		b
m				z
a	z	h	p	s
z	w	z	k	e
y	f	r	n	z

A-Z

LIST ALL THE NAMES OF GOD IN THE ABC'S
YOU KNOW RIGHT NOW

a _____

b _____

c _____

d _____

e _____

f _____

g _____

h _____

i _____

j _____

k _____

l _____

m _____

n _____

o _____

p _____

q _____

r _____

s _____

t _____

u _____

v _____

w _____

x _____

y _____

z _____